CW01640889

The Charities Act 1993 and the PCC

3rd edition

A guide to the SORP 2005 revisions

2006

Guidance on accounts, reports and scrutiny including the Church Accounting Regulations 2006 prescribed by the Business Committee of the General Synod

Church House Publishing
Church House
Great Smith Street
London SW1P 3NZ
Tel: 020 7898 1451
Fax: 020 7898 1449

ISBN-13 978–0–7151–1021 8
ISBN-10 0 7151 1021 7

Published 2006 by Church House Publishing.

Printed in England by
Cromwell Press Ltd,
Trowbridge,
Wiltshire

We acknowledge the support of Ecclesiastical Insurance and Data Developments.

Sponsored by

Contents

Sections that are new or have been revised since the 2001 edition are shown in *italics*

Introduction

Background

This publication is the Church of England's guidance for PCCs to help them comply with Part VI of the Charities Act 1993 and the associated Regulations and also on how best to follow the Charity Commission's revised Statement of Recommended Practice issued in March 2005 (SORP 2005). It also incorporates the Charity Commission's directions for carrying out an independent examination and summarizes, for the convenience of PCCs, the recommendations of the Charities SORP on the way in which a charity should report annually on the resources entrusted to it and the activities it undertakes. The Church is required to follow the law for charities.

The first edition of this guidance was published in 1997. It was produced by a working party set up by the then Central Board of Finance (CBF). The second edition was published in 2001 by the Archbishops' Council Finance Division.

This revision of the PCC Guide has been produced by a sub-group of the Diocesan Accounts Group but will be maintained in the future by the Diocesan Accounts Group itself reporting to the Diocesan Secretaries Liaison Group. The sub-group comprises representation from diocesan and national church staff and external professional advisers. The assistance of Kingston Smith LLP (a firm of accountants) is gratefully acknowledged.

The regime of regulated public accountability

The requirements for PCC reports and accounts are proportionate to the size of the PCC. Smaller PCCs can produce simpler accounts and reports than larger PCCs and only PCCs over the audit threshold (which will increase if the Charities Bill is passed) will need to prepare accounts that fully comply with SORP 2005.

So that all PCCs do not have to obtain and refer to the published law, this guidance contains all the pertinent requirements that most PCCs will need to prepare their accounts. It has been produced to ensure consistency with SORP 2005 and corresponding regulations made under Part VI of the Charities Act 1993.

The purpose of the statutory accounting regime for charities is to build public confidence, and the changes in SORP 2005 are a natural development of the earlier framework. The changes largely concern new accounting standards for the preparation of accounts on the accruals basis and additional stewardship disclosures in the annual report.

The Church Accounting Regulations 2006

The Church Accounting Regulations were made in 1997 and the Church Accounting (Amendment) Regulations were made in 2001. For accounting periods ending on or after 31 December 2006 they have been replaced with the Church Accounting Regulations 2006. These regulations do not contain the level of detail that was present in the previous regulations but require PCCs to follow SORP 2005 and the Charities Act 1993 in preparing their Annual Report and financial statements. The 2006 regulations continue with the existing requirement that all PCCs must have an audit or independent examination, not just those with gross income or total expenditure over £10,000. This assures compliance with the statutory requirements in a format that connects with the requirements of the Church Representation Rules.

How should this book be used?

The treasurer and other members of the PCC are invited to:

- Read and note Chapter 1 on what the law requires and decide which options apply to their particular PCC.
- Refer to the relevant further chapters as indicated in the following flow chart.
- Make sure that others, such as the independent examiner, have access to the information that relates to their work.

Use this chart each year to decide on the format of your annual financial statement and the scrutiny you require

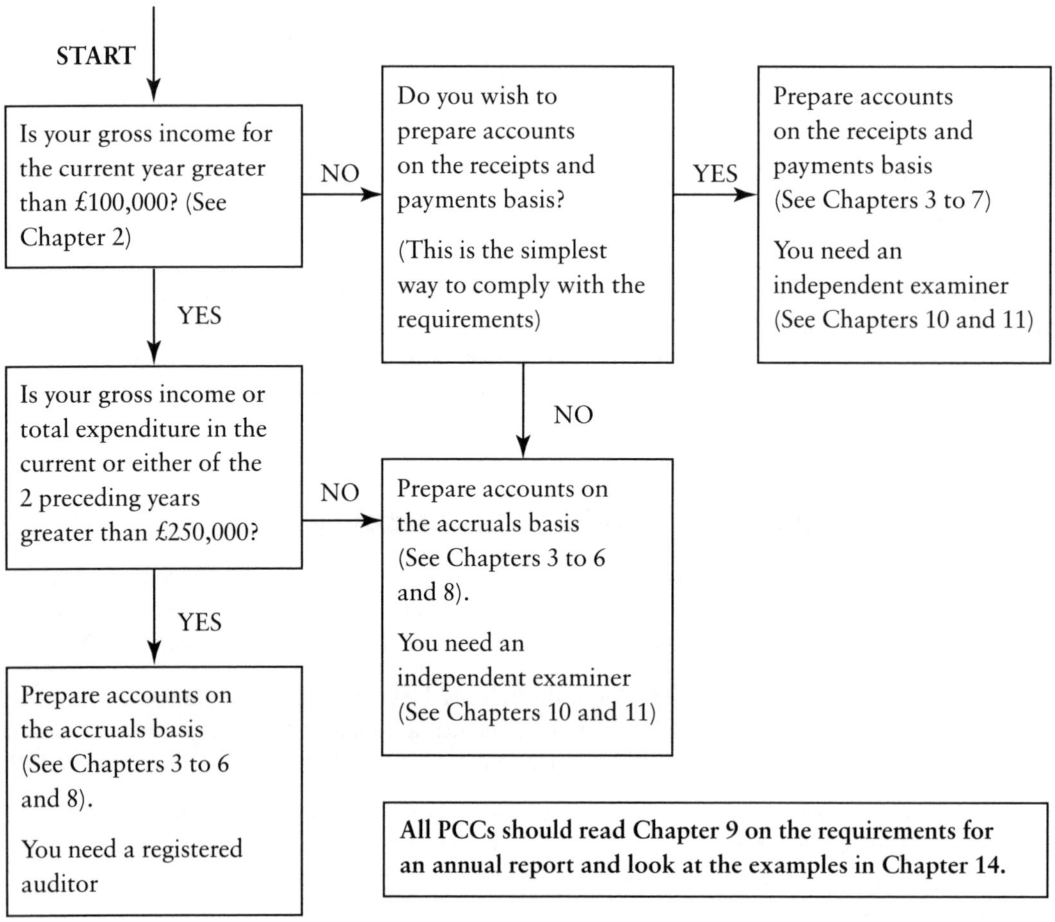

Commencement date

These new requirements come into effect for PCCs for the financial year ending 1 January to 31 December 2006. Accounts will be prepared on the new basis for presentation to Annual Parochial Church Meetings in the spring of 2007. Figures from 2005 accounts will need to be restated.

Abbreviations

The following abbreviations are used in this publication:

AC	Archbishops' Council
APB	Auditing Practices Board
ASB	Accounting Standards Board
CAR	Church Accounting Regulations

CBF	Central Board of Finance
CRRs	Church Representation Rules
DBF	Diocesan Board of Finance
DCC	District Church Council
FRS	Financial Reporting Standard
HMRC	HM Revenue & Customs
PCC	Parochial Church Council
R&P	Receipts and Payments
SOFA	Statement of Financial Activities
SORP	Statement of Recommended Practice

The term 'electoral roll' refers throughout to the church electoral roll of a parish.
The term 'parish' refers throughout to an ecclesiastical parish.

chapter 1

An overview of the law

1.1 This chapter gives an overview of the requirements of the Charities Act 1993 and associated regulations and relates them to both large and small Parochial Church Councils (PCCs) and parishes. It incorporates the revised accounting framework that was introduced by the Charities SORP 2005 for accounts that are prepared for the year ending 31 December 2006 and following years.

Introduction

1.2 The accounting, auditing and reporting regime for almost all charities, including Church of England PCCs, is contained in Part VI of the Charities Act 1993. The Charities (Accounts and Reports) Regulations 1995, which implemented Part VI of the Act, and The Charities (Accounts and Reports) Regulations 2000 were replaced by the Charities (Accounts and Reports) Regulations 2005 for accounting periods beginning after 31 March 2005.

1.3 The law makes it clear that charities are accountable to the public for the resources they control. The Charity Accounting Regulations seek to provide a regime in which charitable organizations receiving funds for public benefit are able to demonstrate to the public that they have observed the trust placed in them in the handling and use of those funds. The Regulations require that charities' activities are fully disclosed to the public, and specifically require charities to prepare their accounts in accordance with the Charities SORP which is issued by the Charity Commission as an Accounting Standards Board SORP making body.

1.4 The latest Statement of Recommended Practice on Accounting and Reporting by Charities was issued by the Charity Commission in March 2005, and is referred to as 'SORP 2005'. It supersedes the previous SORP issued in October 2000. By preparing accounts in accordance with SORP 2005, charities will have met the requirements of the accounting formats and contents in the Act and the Charity Accounting Regulations.

1.5 PCCs are currently excepted charities and do not have to file annual returns or annual reports and accounts with the Charity Commission (see paras 1.33 and 1.34). However, they do have to prepare their annual financial statements as if they were registered. The accounts must conform to the Charities Act 1993 and the Charity Accounting Regulations, and, as with any other charity, PCCs must make them available to the public.

1.6 To assist PCCs it was decided to draw up this guidance specifically tailored to the needs of PCCs within the requirements of the Church Representation Rules (CRRs). By following them PCCs meet the requirements of the Charities Act 1993, the Charity Accounting Regulations and Charities SORP.

Accounting framework

1.7 The general accounting framework for charities in England and Wales (into which a PCC's financial statements are required to fit) is set out in a number of publications. These are:

- **Part VI of the Charities Act 1993;**
- **The Charities (Accounts and Reports) Regulations 2005;**
- **The Statement of Recommended Practice** 'Accounting and Reporting by Charities' (SORP 2005) issued by the Charity Commission in March 2005;
- **Accounting and Financial Reporting Standards** issued or adopted by the Accounting Standards Board (ASB), which are applicable to accounts prepared on the accruals basis and intended to show a true and fair view.

1.8 The requirements concerning accounts and external scrutiny are graduated according to the size of the charity. PCCs must follow regulations set out in:

- **The Charities Act;**
- **The PCCs (Powers) Measure 1956;**
- **The Church Representation Rules** (CRRs);
- **The Church Accounting Regulations 2006,** which form the link between the CRRs and the requirements of the Act.

1.9 The Church Accounting Regulations 2006 provide:

- A legal framework for PCC accounting and annual reporting, which requires PCCs to follow SORP 2005 and the Charities Act 1993 in the preparation of their annual reports and financial statements. The format of the financial statements will be either:

  – accruals accounts consisting of a comprehensive 'Statement of Financial Activities' (SOFA) as the basis of accounts, providing analysis of all incoming resources and the application of resources, together with a balance sheet and explanatory notes (all compulsory for larger PCCs);

  or alternatively (at the option of smaller PCCs):

  – a R&P Account for each fund, together with a Statement of Assets and Liabilities.

  The details concerning the format of the annual report and financial statements are covered in this guidance and are no longer contained in the Regulations.

- A statutory requirement for external scrutiny of all PCC accounts, in the form of:

  – audit by a registered auditor (compulsory for the largest PCCs);

  or alternatively:

  – less rigorous 'independent examination' for smaller PCCs.

General guidance

1.10 This publication is aimed at all PCCs and is intended to draw together comprehensively all the Regulations and guidance they will generally need in preparing their accounts and having them subjected to external scrutiny. However, the Archbishops' Council is also publishing a shorter guide which will be suitable and sufficient for those 11,000 PCCs who need only to prepare accounts on a Receipts & Payments (R&P) basis.

1.11 It also provides guidance for the selection of independent examiners and explains their duties. This will assist individuals who undertake independent examinations of PCC accounts. However, those who undertake the audit or independent examination of PCC accounts will, for their own purposes, need to refer elsewhere for detailed information and guidance about their statutory rights and duties.

1.12 Those larger PCCs whose gross income is greater than £100,000 may need to consider the other documents mentioned in para. 1.7, particularly SORP 2005, especially when required to deal with more complex accounting issues such as branches and investment assets.

1.13 Since this publication represents extracts from other and more detailed documents, there will be matters that some PCCs will encounter that are not addressed within it. In these instances reference will need to be made to those more detailed documents. However, this publication is as comprehensive and as universally applicable as it can reasonably be.

The bases for accounts and scrutiny

1.14 The accounting framework provides for two separate bases for preparing and reporting on annual accounts, which depend upon the size of the PCC in terms of its gross income and, for certain purposes, its total expenditure for the year.

1.15 All PCCs exceeding £100,000 gross income per year must prepare accounts using the accruals basis, incorporating a Statement of Financial Activities, a balance sheet and notes to the accounts in accordance with the Regulations. Their accounts must, therefore, conform to the statutory requirements of the Regulations to provide a 'true and fair' view of the PCC's incoming resources, application of resources and state of affairs in financial terms.

1.16 For PCCs under the audit threshold (currently with neither gross income nor total expenditure exceeding £250,000 per year for any of the current and the two preceding years), a statutory form of external scrutiny of their accounts is required and may be either by independent examination or by audit. PCCs exceeding this threshold must have a statutory audit by a registered auditor.

1.17 All PCCs under the accruals accounts threshold (with gross income for the year not exceeding £100,000) can elect to prepare accounts on the R&P basis. Such accounts are not subject to any detailed regulations but should follow the guidance given in Chapter 7. External scrutiny of the accounts is required but this would normally take the form of independent examination rather than audit.

1.18 There is no statutory requirement in the Charities Act for an independent examination where a PCC's gross income and total expenditure for the year in question are below £10,000. However, the Church Accounting Regulations 2006 and the Church Representation Rules require an examination by an independent examiner and the statutory requirements for carrying out the examination can be used as an outline guide.

Teams, united benefices and pluralities

1.19 The general principle to keep in mind is that statutory accounts must be produced for the legal entity. That means that PCCs (as the legal entity) must prepare appropriate annual reports and accounts that are in accordance with the Act and, for accruals accounts, the Charities Accounts Regulations, and this responsibility cannot be delegated to others.

1.20 This is quite straightforward in most cases but questions arise when considering teams, united benefices and pluralities.

United benefices and pluralities

1.21 In the case of united benefices and pluralities, each PCC must produce accounts in the statutory format. The thresholds are tested for each PCC, which must each appoint an independent examiner or, if appropriate, an auditor. Providing the independence test holds good, the same person may agree to serve more than one PCC.

Teams

1.22 Teams vary a great deal and the guidance on how to meet the requirements of the Charities Act varies with the circumstances. For example:

(a) Teams which comprise a number of separate PCCs must produce separate accounts that meet the statutory requirements at the level of each PCC. Of course a summary financial statement can be produced at the level of the team, but there is no requirement to do so and there are no constraints on the format.

(b) Other teams may have been formed on the basis of a single parish and PCC with more than one place of worship but without DCCs. As before, accounts that meet the statutory requirements must be produced for the PCC. Of course there is nothing to stop the production of supplementary financial statements that relate to the different congregations but there is no requirement to do so and there are no constraints on the format. It may be appropriate for such information to take the form of notes to the accounts (so that they are part of that body of information).

Situations where DCCs are in place

1.23 Teams (often in urban areas) may comprise a single parish and PCC in which there are highly developed DCCs. The 'mother church' may now be a matter of history and the 'daughter' churches have a maturity of their own and appear to be independent. It is possible that the team rectorship moves between the churches.

1.24 A similar situation arises (often in rural areas) where pastoral re-organization has combined former parishes into a single benefice and PCC, with DCCs to retain the sense of local community where there were formerly separate parishes.

1.25 In both these cases statutory accounts must be produced at the level of the PCC. Depending on local circumstances this may not be a contentious matter because the accounts may always have been prepared at PCC level. Where DCCs have traditionally prepared financial statements there is understandable concern that the statutory requirements of the financial regime are seen to replace and be preferred over the local pastoral needs.

1.26 While certain responsibilities can be passed down from the PCC to DCCs, this is not the case with financial responsibility which must by law stay with the PCC. DCCs cannot hold assets, they do not have body corporate status and they should not be taking financial decisions and signing contracts. Of course the PCC can decide that DCCs can operate within an agreed budget but the PCC is the only legal entity that is able to enter into a contract.

1.27 Where DCCs have been preparing their own accounts there is no reason why this should not continue, but these accounts, until brought together at the PCC level, are non-statutory and careful co-ordination between the DCCs and the PCC over the final examination/audit of the PCC accounts will be needed.

Aggregation

1.28 If the DCCs have been used to preparing their own, separate accounts, the need to aggregate the accounts at PCC level may be a cause for concern. Consideration of the following may mitigate the circumstances:

- If the DCCs are very small and the PCC of which they form a part is below the accruals accounts threshold, the statutory requirements should be relatively easily met by taking R&P accounts for the individual DCCs and stapling them together with summary statements of receipts and payments and statements of assets and liabilities. An annual report will be required at PCC level which could have general details for the PCC and short reports from each DCC.

- If the aggregated gross income exceeds £100,000 then the statutory requirement is for a single statement of accounts on the accruals basis covering all the DCCs and other transactions at PCC level. Endowment funds would need to be included.

- Instances of the £250,000 threshold being exceeded and requiring an audit are likely to be rare and, where they occur, manageable.

- The independent examiner's task may appear onerous but the person responsible for the examination does not have to carry it all out themselves. The PCC will need to appoint an independent examiner (who will need to meet the requirements of the task) but they might delegate aspects of the work to others, particularly if a number of congregations have to be covered. In this way each DCC may have its part of the aggregated accounts examined, but the examiners would be working to the PCC's overall examiner, who will take overall responsibility for any work they have delegated by agreeing the programme of work of local examiners, reviewing their work and reporting on the overall accounts of the PCC.

1.29 It cannot be avoided that aggregation at PCC level may increase the gross income or total expenditure of the PCC to a level which means that it crosses a threshold and enters a more rigorous regime.

1.30 It should be noted that a PCC with DCCs does not require a common bank account. The PCC may arrange for each DCC to have its own bank account but this will need to be subject to the overall control of the PCC and subject to an assessment of any risks and benefits.

1.31 Some groups of PCCs operate a group or benefice account, to which PCCs contribute. It is used to fund joint activities, such as the incumbent's working expenses or a magazine. This fund may be accounted for in one of two ways:

(i) One PCC in the group may control the fund as a restricted fund and receive grants from the other PCCs in the group. This PCC then accounts for the fund and the other PCCs show their contribution as a grant. If the fund is a significant sum of money, the PCC may not wish to adopt this method as it may move them into a more complex accounting regime.

(ii) The joint account may be handled as a 'joint venture', where each PCC accounts for its share of the total fund. A PCC treasurer may operate an account, which serves the joint activity. The expenditure on the account should be allocated appropriately to each PCC. The PCC treasurer running the account should not treat payments received from the other PCCs as income. Any assets or liabilities generated within the account also need to be allocated to each PCC at the year-end.

The duties of the PCC

1.32 The PCC is responsible for all parish finance, its management and control, including the appointment of a treasurer. While it may delegate some of its duties (for example, to DCCs), this does not remove its legal responsibilities. These include:

(a) Keeping 'proper accounting records', which must be sufficient to show and explain all the PCC's transactions. The records, together with the annual financial statements, must be preserved for at least six years from the end of the financial year to which they relate. The records must be sufficient to:

(i) show and explain all the PCC's transactions;

(ii) disclose the PCC's financial position at any time with reasonable accuracy;

(iii) enable the required accounts to be prepared;

(iv) show on a day-to-day basis all receipts and payments and what they were for;

(v) include a record of all assets and liabilities.

(b) Ensuring that the finances of the PCC are under its control and only delegated if the PCC can ensure that its wishes will be followed.

(c) Preparing an annual account (financial statements) and report, which shall be presented to the Annual Parochial Church Meeting in accordance with the requirements of the Church Representation Rules.

(d) Arranging for a suitable independent examination or audit of the financial statements.

Excepted status

1.33 PCCs are currently excepted by Statutory Instrument from registration with the Charity Commission. The exception expires at the end of September 2007. The Charities Bill (before parliament at the time of writing) is likely to require PCCs with gross income exceeding £100,000 to register with the Charity Commission. Some PCCs that have already registered voluntarily must also comply with the requirements for registered charities.

1.34 As a result of the exception, PCCs do not currently have a charity registration number and do not have to file an annual report and accounts with the Commission unless specifically requested. These must, however, (under the Church Representation Rules) be sent to the Secretary of the Diocesan Board of Finance. They must also be provided to the public upon written request. PCCs are still charitable bodies and may, inter alia, claim tax refunds on Gift Aid contributions, receive investment income without deduction of income tax and in general enjoy all the other tax reliefs available to registered charities.

Basic overview – PCCs must:

- record their incoming resources and the investment or expenditure of their resources in three main categories: unrestricted funds, restricted funds and endowment funds;
- aggregate the accounts of other parts of the organization which the PCC controls;
- account for their stewardship of those resources
  - *either* in cash-based accounts, consisting of receipts and payments account(s) with a Statement of Assets and Liabilities
  - *or* in accruals accounts which show a true and fair view, consisting of a Statement of Financial Activities, a balance sheet and notes to give certain additional information;
- identify and, if accruals accounts are prepared, value their assets, to help the public to understand the PCC's financial position;
- report on their finances and activities in such a way that the general public can understand what has been going on;
- have the accounts scrutinized by an independent examiner or audited by a registered auditor.

Good presentation points

Financial statements should be transparent so that they may be easily understood.

- **Avoid too much detail**

  Detailed analyses of all the individual accounts, even in the smallest parishes, can be confusing. Only make reference to what is material and round all figures to the nearest pound.

- **Summarize where possible**

  Summarizing different funds in columnar format gives the reader a better overall picture. It also allows a reduction in the number of comparative figures.

- **Prepare a summarized account**

  A summary, derived from the full financial statements, may be produced to help parishioners understand the finances. There are rules about the preparation of summaries in the Charities SORP, which recommends that information about the Statement of Financial Activities and the balance sheet should be included. The full annual report and financial statements should always be available, however.

- **Put detail in the notes**

  The reader is less likely to be confused by the details when looking at the overall picture.

chapter 2

Making the choice

2.1 This chapter describes whether accounts on the R&P or accruals accounting basis must or may be prepared.

How large is your PCC?

2.2 In order to discover which aspects of the Regulations apply to the PCC, its statutory 'gross income' and 'total expenditure' must first be calculated according to the Charity Commission's rules. The PCC can then identify where it stands in the accounting framework described in Chapter 1.

What is the 'gross income' of the PCC?

2.3 The gross income is the total recorded income of the PCC in all unrestricted and restricted funds but not amounts received as capital (endowment) funds, nor as capital gains. Gross income should be recorded before the deduction of any costs or expenses and includes the following (the list of items in Chapter 6 will help to identify income items).

- Voluntary receipts
- Gross proceeds of activities for generating funds
- Investment receipts
- Receipts from charitable activities and
- Any expendable endowment spent or transferred to income funds and any unapplied total return allocated or transferred to income funds during the year (this latter is unlikely to arise in the context of small or unendowed charities).

2.4 The following items should be **excluded**:

- a loan received by the PCC;
- the repayment to the PCC of a loan made by them;
- the proceeds of the sale of investments or 'functional fixed assets' (such as a hall or curate's house, which are held for the purpose of furthering the mission of the church) or any gain or profit on their sale;
- donations received by the PCC with the specific requirement that they be held as endowments (i.e. the income can be used by the PCC and would be shown above, but the primary endowment would not be included).

If the calculation of statutory gross income is being made from financial statements prepared on the accruals basis, then any unrealized gains shown as arising from the revaluation of either investment assets or any functional fixed assets used for the work of the PCC should be **excluded**.

What is the 'total expenditure' of the PCC?

2.5 This is the total gross expenditure by the PCC from all funds, including the endowment funds. The list of items in Chapter 6 will help to identify expenditure items.

2.6 The following should be **excluded:**

- the making of a loan;
- the repayment of a loan by the PCC;
- the purchase of investments and 'functional fixed assets' (such as a hall or curate's house, which are held for the purpose of furthering the mission of the church) or any loss on their sale;
- any transfers between income funds.

If the calculation of statutory total expenditure is being made from financial statements prepared on the accruals basis, then any unrealized losses shown as arising from the revaluation of investment assets or any fixed assets used for the work of the PCC (other than a provision for permanent diminution in value of the latter kind of asset) should be **excluded**.

Exclusions

2.7 In calculating the gross income, there should be no netting off of expenditure and income (no cancelling income against expenditure). Suppose the parish runs a fete and raises £1,000 after charging £500 for expenses. They should show £1,500 of income and £500 of expenditure. If the netting off is small (not material), say the expenses were only £50, then this requirement to 'gross' up can be ignored.

2.8 If in doubt, include an item rather than leave it out. The new rules are to help people to understand the financial statements more easily and to help PCCs have the information they need for managing their affairs properly. These aims should be kept in mind when deciding which small items should be included or excluded, either gross or net.

2.9 Insurance claims are indemnity payments and may be netted off against expenditure to the extent that they do not include a profit or gain element (e.g. 'new for old' or 'rainy day' insurance). Where the insurer pays a supplier's bill direct (as is often the case with vehicle damage claims) that amount should not be shown as a payment nor a receipt.

2.10 Money may be received to build a new building or to improve an existing building. If the funds raised create an endowment (due to the nature of the gift) or the asset to be improved is an endowment asset the funds raised are endowment and should be excluded from the calculation of gross income.

2.11 If there is a major appeal for activities or repair or a major legacy is received in a year it will be quite possible for the gross income and total expenditure in that year to increase from, say, £50,000 to over £100,000. If this happens, no attempt must be made to manipulate the figures by artificially accelerating or delaying activities. As the PCC will be handling larger sums of money it is only right that it should have to account for them in a more rigorous way.

2.12 The law requires all gross income and total expenditure to be included, even if its inclusion makes the financial size of the parish much bigger than was previously the case and than the PCC expects. The calculations are made to arrive at a figure of genuine gross income and total expenditure – the amount of money that the PCC is handling every year – and not just the amount of money it has to spend after the deduction of regular expenses.

How to use gross income and total expenditure

2.13 Most PCCs have a comparatively small gross income, well below £100,000. Provided their gross income is below £100,000 they can choose to prepare R&P accounts and a Statement of Assets and Liabilities, although they are free to decide to prepare full accruals accounts, which must then be prepared in accordance with the SORP. However, these PCCs will need to make sure which category they are in if they are given a large sum of money (perhaps a legacy) or if they engage in major fund-raising for a particular activity project.

2.14 Once a PCC has exceeded the audit threshold (currently gross income or total expenditure of £250,000), it will need to have its financial statements audited by a registered auditor for the year in which the threshold is exceeded and for the following two years, even if the threshold is not exceeded in those two years. PCCs should therefore check their gross income and total expenditure figures over the two previous years in order to ascertain whether the threshold of £250,000 has been exceeded for either income or expenditure in any of the three years, in which case a full audit would be required.

2.15 Any parish that, for some reason, has a small statutory gross income (under £100,000) but a large statutory total expenditure (over £250,000) is allowed by charity law to prepare R&P accounts but will have to have them audited.

Examples of the thresholds with minimum requirements

* compulsory # the PCC can opt for

	income	*expenditure*	*accounts*	*examination*	*reason*
Year 1:	£50,000	£49,000	R&P #	ind exam #	
Year 2:	£85,000	£51,000	R&P #	ind exam #	fund-raising
Year 3:	£105,000	£53,000	accruals *	ind exam #	fund-raising
Year 4:	£60,000	£130,000	R&P #	ind exam #	major roof repair
Year 5:	£62,000	£58,000	R&P #	ind exam #	
Year 6:	£63,000	£61,000	R&P #	ind exam #	

In year 3 full accruals accounts have to be prepared because the fund-raising moved the PCC over the £100,000 gross income threshold. The PCC could return to R&P accounts the following year when the income dropped, but it would be wise (though not compulsory) for the PCC to continue to prepare accruals accounts while it was handling a large expenditure on, say, a major building repair.

	income	*expenditure*	*accounts*	*examination*	*reason*
Year 1:	£150,000	£149,000	accruals *	ind exam #	
Year 2:	£260,000	£151,000	accruals *	audit *	Heritage grant
Year 3:	£160,000	£155,000	accruals *	audit *	
Year 4:	£165,000	£280,000	accruals *	audit *	rebuilding
Year 5:	£172,000	£158,000	accruals *	audit *	
Year 6:	£178,000	£161,000	accruals *	audit *	
Year 7:	£184,000	£166,000	accruals *	ind exam #	

In year 2 and the following two years an audit was required because the gross income exceeded the £250,000 threshold. Again the threshold was exceeded in the total expenditure in year 4, which required an audit in years 5 and 6 as well. With the rebuilding programme over, the PCC could revert to independent examination in year 7.

Summary of threshold calculations for accounts on the Receipts and Payments basis

The following should be included:

Gross income

- Voluntary income from donations (including any related gift aid tax reclaims) grants, gifts and legacies (see Note 1 below);
- Gross proceeds from fund-raising and other trading activities undertaken for generating funds;
- Investment income (including interest, dividends, related tax reclaims and rents);
- Gross proceeds from the sale of goods or services in furtherance of the charity's objectives; and
- The amount of any expendable endowment spent or transferred to income funds and where a charity operates a total return approach to investment of capital funds the amount of any unapplied total return or transferred to income funds during the year (see Note 2 below).

Total expenditure

- Costs of generating funds, including fund raising, trading activities, investment property costs and investment management fees;
- Charitable expenditure in furtherance of the objects of the charity including:
- Grants and donations payable;
- Support costs; and
- Governance and management and administration costs of the charity.

The following should be excluded:

- Receipt of a loan by the charity;
- Loan repayments to the charity;
- Proceeds, gains or profits on sale or disposal of investments and functional fixed assets; and
- Actuarial gains on any defined benefit pension scheme.

- Granting of a loan;
- Repayment of a loan;
- Purchase of investments and functional fixed assets;
- Losses on disposal of investments and functional fixed assets; and
- Actuarial losses on any defined benefit pension scheme.

Note 1: Any gifts or donations which the donor expects will be, or may be, retained for investment or ongoing use by the charity are capital (endowment), and should be excluded.

Note 2: Any allocation of unapplied total return will only affect endowed charities that have obtained a consent order from the Charity Commission to operate a total return approach to investments.

chapter 3

How should the PCC account for its funds?

3.1 This chapter is relevant to all PCCs. It describes the nature of the different funds the PCC will hold so that they can be separated in the records and the financial statements to demonstrate that the PCC has observed the specific terms of trust attaching to those funds.

Funds

3.2 The PCC may allocate certain sums of money to particular funds for particular purposes or it may raise funds for particular purposes. The following are examples of the names of some of these funds which may have grown up over the years:

General Fund	Bell Fund
Church Restoration Fund	Choir & Organ Fund
Church Hall Fund	Legacies Fund
General Bequest Fund	Sunday School Fund
Building Fund	Mission & Charities Fund
Fabric Fund	Churchyard Fund
Flower Fund	Maintenance Reserve Fund

In addition there may be funds in the name of the person who gave or left the money, possibly for a particular purpose. This chapter will show that legacies should be treated in the same way as other donations, subject to specific rules about recognizing legacies for financial statements prepared on the accruals basis.

3.3 Each of these funds is associated with a particular purpose or, in the case of some legacies, with the source of the funds. But the funds do not immediately tell the reader of the financial statements whether they are held by the PCC in a trust for a particular purpose.

3.4 The word 'fund' has an additional meaning in charity accounting. As well as referring to money allocated for a particular purpose, it also refers to whether the money is restricted for that purpose. With this latter meaning, each fund is legally either unrestricted or restricted, the latter being either income or capital (endowment) in nature. It is important to know the difference between these types of fund as PCCs have to observe clear distinctions between them.

3.5 As stated above, many PCCs will already distinguish between funds because of the purpose to which they have been earmarked (such as those in the list above). For some, a change will be needed merely to record whether the fund is restricted (and if so, whether it is endowed) or unrestricted (and, if so, to confirm its status if designated for a particular purpose) in order to demonstrate that the PCC has properly exercised the trust placed in it.

3.6 PCC members and members of the parish on the Church electoral rolls have been used to financial statements that have been project-based, focusing on where the money has come from and on what activities the Church has spent it. For example, the receipts and payments for the parish magazine, the church hall and similar activities have been shown separately so the reader of the financial statements could see whether each activity was a source of funds or a drain on resources. The charity accounting framework requires fund-based financial statements that enable the reader to see that the PCC is spending funds on the purposes for which they have been given. It may be helpful to give the project-based information, which is not required by law, either in a note to the financial statements or in the annual report (e.g. 'sales of the parish magazine exceeded printing costs by £140'). Even if not given in the financial statements, such information is likely to be important for the PCC in carrying out its responsibilities, and it may be appropriate to report such information in the 'Performance and Achievements' section of the annual report (see Chapter 9).

Unrestricted funds

3.7 All PCCs have a fund, normally called a General Fund, which they use to pay all the everyday expenses. This fund is 'unrestricted' because the money has been given to the Church on the general understanding that it will be used at the discretion of the PCC for furthering the mission and ministry of the Church. Unless specified otherwise, all the money received by the Church is put into the General Fund. Income generated from assets held in an unrestricted fund will be unrestricted income.

3.8 The PCC may decide to put some of the unrestricted fund money aside in other funds for use in the future (for example, for future building repairs). This money is 'designated' for these particular projects for administration purposes only. Designated funds are still unrestricted and can be moved to other general funds (re-designated or un-designated) if the PCC so decides.

Restricted funds

3.9 PCCs also receive money which has been given for a particular purpose, for example:

(i) a collection in church may be announced as being for a particular purpose (such as the purchase of new hymn books, or the repair of the tower;

(ii) a fund-raising event (such as a rummage sale or a coffee morning) may be held for a particular purpose;

(iii) a donation may have been made or a legacy may have been left to the church for a particular purpose (such as the upkeep of the churchyard or the repair of the fabric).

All these sums have been restricted by the donor for a particular purpose and they cannot, and must not, be used by the PCC for any other purpose unless determined by the courts or the Charity Commission. Income generated from assets held in a restricted fund will generally be subject to the same restrictions as the fund.

3.10 An oral or written appeal or a collection for a special purpose, such as the fabric fund, will restrict the income to that purpose. There may be times when more money is raised than is needed for the particular purpose of the appeal. This excess money is restricted to the purpose and should be retained for use for the same purpose, or returned to the donors.

3.11 This situation can be eased if the PCC acquires the power beforehand to use any surpluses for other purposes. The easiest way to avoid any problem is by announcing at the time of the appeal that any unused balance will be put to the general purposes of the PCC. The restriction then applies until the purpose of the appeal has been satisfied. (A general notice to this effect can be placed prominently in the church to catch all occasions.) If someone wants to make a significant donation for a particular purpose, the donor could be asked to specify that they give the PCC permission to use it for alternative purposes under certain conditions.

3.12 There could also be a potential problem if insufficient funds are raised for a particular purpose and the shortfall cannot be made good out of general funds. The PCC should always make clear in appeals what it would do if this situation arose – for example, to return all the donations or to use them for another related purpose.

3.13 When special collections are made to send straight off to other charities (eg Christian Aid, missionary societies) and the nature of the appeal is that there is no discretion for the PCC to do anything other than send the money directly to the charity, these are not funds of the PCC and should not be included in the PCC's gross income or total expenditure. It is good practice to include a list of these collections in the PCC's accounts, if only to show to the congregation how money has been collected and sent off.

Endowment funds

3.14 Another form of restricted fund is known as an endowment fund. This is either money given to the Church with the specific instruction that only the income gained from the money can be spent, or an asset (such as a house) donated to be retained for continuing use by the Church. The original money or assets (the 'capital') cannot normally be spent and must remain in the form of equivalent assets (such as a house) or investments, but not necessarily the same asset that was given. It may be in a fund that is named after the donor.

3.15 There are two types of endowment fund, which must be distinguished in accruals accounts by note:

(i) **permanent:**
a particular type of restricted fund where the capital, in accordance with the explicit requirements of the founding donor, must be held permanently (the PCC have no power to convert it into income and spend it like other income). Any return generated by the endowment (e.g. dividends) should be spent as determined by the donor.

(ii) **expendable:**
an endowment fund where the capital may, in certain circumstances, be spent. (The PCC have this power, if given by the donor. This fund is not income when it is first received because there is no duty on the part of the PCC to apply it for its purposes. However, if the power to convert is used, then at that time the amount converted becomes income.) Any return generated by the endowment will be spent as determined by the donor.

3.16 Any expenses incurred in the administration of the capital fund (such as the fees of the person who manages the investments) should be charged against the capital of the fund. However, if the trust establishing a fund provides for it or if the capital fund has insufficient to meet such costs or cannot be used (e.g. they are land or buildings), they can be charged against other unrestricted PCC funds (normally the general fund).

Accounting for different types of fund

3.17 Where a PCC holds funds, other than unrestricted funds, its accounting records must be adequate to allow separate accounts to be produced for each fund. Restricted and endowment funds must be shown separately in the annual financial statements and PCCs should also be able to account separately for any funds they have designated.

3.18 In the accounting records this can be done either by using separate columns in the cash book for the different types of fund or by clearly labelling each entry to distinguish those that are unrestricted and those that are restricted or designated.

3.19 In the annual financial statements unrestricted, restricted and endowment funds must be reported separately. As a minimum all funds of one type should be reported together, either as three separate columns or, in the case of accounts on the R&P basis, as three separate statements of account (see example Receipts & Payments Accounts). It is important that the reader can tell that all the funds are not held on the same basis and it is important that the PCC members know that certain funds have restrictions on the way the money can be used. The PCC must also be able to demonstrate that it still holds assets belonging to restricted and endowment funds and has not used these for unauthorized purposes. It is a breach of trust to spend restricted funds for purposes other than for which they were given without the prior consent of the Charity Commission.

3.20 The PCC's unused monies may be invested and investment income generated. Any income earned belongs to the fund whose assets were invested and the income is, therefore, subject to the same restrictions as that fund. So the investment income must be attributed to each fund, based on the amounts invested and the time for which they were invested and must be accounted for as part of the fund to which they belonged.

3.21 The only exceptions to this are:

(i) where the donor has expressly provided for some other use for the income;

(ii) where the asset is part of a permanent endowment held for general purposes. In this case the capital is restricted in an endowment fund (because it cannot be spent) but the income is unrestricted since it can be spent for the PCC's general purposes.

3.22 If a restricted fund has assets (e.g. a house or investments) and any are sold, the proceeds of sale must be held within the same restricted fund.

3.23 SORP 2005 makes it clear that funds may be grouped and sub-analysed by major fund in the notes to the financial statements, and so all endowments may be reported on as one group, all other restricted funds as another group and all funds with no restriction as a third group. On the R&P basis the PCC should produce either a separate R&P account for every restricted fund or a combined account that adequately distinguishes the different funds by grouping and sub-analysing them in the same way.

3.24 In some cases other bodies of trustees may hold funds from which the PCC is legally entitled to benefit. If such trustees are only the custodians (i.e. they have no discretion over the use of the fund) then that money is a fund (in most cases an endowment fund) of the PCC. If the PCC does not have enough discretion over the use of the funds to make it the 'charity trustee' of those funds, then they should not be accounted for in the PCC's financial statements. Instead, the fact of the fund's existence, its purpose and the legal restrictions on the PCC's entitlement should be included in the notes to the financial statements as a connected charity.

3.25 With parishes bearing an increasingly larger part of the burden of maintaining the Church of England it may seem odd to think that there may be parishes who have received income which they may find difficult to spend. Usually these will relate to restricted funds. Some examples might include the following:

- The PCC has investments in a restricted fund which are the proceeds of a house used for curates and parish staff in the past. This may be from a period in between employment of one staff member and another when a house has been bought in which it is possible that the parish is subsequently not required to house a worker; the PCC will then have to consider what to do with the fund.
- A building appeal fund has been set up but because the proper permissions have not yet been granted there is some doubt whether the project will go ahead.
- Money has been specifically raised to send an individual to do a specific project in a third world country but because of a recent civil war that person cannot go.

The status of such funds should be explained in the notes to the financial statements and any proposed action to dispose of the unexpended balances should be disclosed. This may include returning funds to the donors, or obtaining permission (either from the donors or by order of the Charity Commission) for the funds to be spent on other purposes.

How already established funds should be handled

3.26 Because restricted, endowment and unrestricted funds may not have been separated prior to the Charities Act 1993, some PCCs will have had funds of the different types mixed together under one heading. The composition of these fund balances may have become lost due to the passage of time. There might have been no way of telling accurately how much of the money in a fund was restricted, or endowment and how much was designated. For example, the fabric fund may include unrestricted money designated to the fund by the PCC over the years and restricted money raised through a specific appeal or fund-raising activity.

3.27 The obligation to keep restricted, endowment and unrestricted funds separate has been a tenet of trust law for many years. The fact that these funds had not been separately accounted for was addressed in the first edition of this guidance. The Charities Act 1993 did not introduce any new law in this respect.

3.28 In the first edition of this guidance it was stated that the PCC has a duty to research the composition of the funds from the available records and it needs to go back at least the seven years (six plus the current year) that was enshrined in the 1960 Charities Act for the retention of records, which is consolidated in the 1993 Charities Act. The research and its results should be formally minuted, and shown to the examiner (or auditor) of the financial statements. If there is no evidence of unspent restricted funds (or eroded endowments) then no further action is necessary. If there is such evidence, but it is insufficient to establish the facts, the opinion of a professional accountant or a lawyer may be necessary. If there is evidence that endowment has been spent, then ratification by the Charity Commission may be necessary. The Commission has power to approve capital spending of endowments which produce less than £1,000 annual income. If PCCs are in doubt about this, they should seek advice from the Charity Commission. All PCCs should have addressed these matters and completed the research.

3.29 As the way in which funds are handled will be important for a proper understanding of accruals accounts, the notes to the financial statements should include a brief description of the purpose of major funds within the financial statements.

Tips for handling different funds

- Clear records of restricted money should be kept so that it can readily be identified. Poor records can lead to confused administration and then it is possible that the rules will be ignored and restricted and unrestricted funds will be merged with one another.
- Restricting money by specifying the objects when making an appeal has two advantages:

  (i) As restricted money can only be used for the purpose for which it was given, it cannot be 'raided' for other purposes.

  (ii) People tend to give more to funds that are restricted to a particular purpose with which they can readily identify.
- Expenditure of restricted funds may anticipate promised funding at the time the expenditure is incurred. It is acceptable practice in such cases to show a deficit on the project and then wait for the promised funding before deciding what balance must be met from the general fund. However, any insufficiency of the general fund for this purpose cannot be made good out of other restricted funds. Where material, deficit balances on restricted funds should be shown separately on the face of the balance sheet, and not netted off against other restricted fund balances. Details will also need to be given in the annual report (see Chapter 9).
- Collections at some funerals are taken in a bowl by the church door and are taken by the undertaker for a specific purpose at the wish of the bereaved family. These collections should only be recorded and accounted for by the PCC if the money is given directly to the Church or the PCC makes the decision as to the use to which it should be put.
- Fees for the services of the clergy, bell ringers, organists, vergers or choir at weddings and for clergy, organists, vergers and gravediggers at funerals, need not be included in the financial statements if the money is paid over in full directly to those involved. In this case the PCC is acting as an intermediary and these fees do not count towards PCC income. If a choir fund is built up with some of the choir fees (e.g. to pay for outings or social events), this is the property of the choir and is not a PCC fund.
- PCCs will from time to time collect money on behalf of other charities in a public place or in church services. Examples of this include Christmas carolling and Christian Aid door-to-door collections. In these instances these receipts are not to be included in the PCC's income as the PCC is acting as an agent for the charity. This is the case whether the money collected is sent off to the charity or if the money is counted and the PCC treasurer writes out a cheque for money paid into its bank account. Although the item must not be included in the SOFA there should be a note in the annual report or the financial statements to say that the PCC was acting in this way. If any such funds are held in the PCC's bank account at the year-end the accounts should show a liability to the charity(ies) concerned.
- PCCs should remember that they do not have to accept a gift if they are uncertain of its source or if they are not happy at abiding by the donor's conditions. All gifts for which the PCC reclaims tax under the Gift Aid scheme must be shown in the financial statements and its use agreed by the PCC. This would include the situation where tax is reclaimed on a donation paid by Gift Aid to be used for the PCC's charitable purposes at the minister's discretion.
- There is no formal reason why PCCs should agree to accept every gift but written evidence of gifts and their restrictions should be obtained wherever possible.
- Legacies given for the general purposes of the PCC should immediately be credited to the general fund. Unless the donor has restricted the use of the legacy in the Will, it remains unrestricted and may not be restricted by the PCC. All or a part of the legacy may then be designated for a particular purpose but it should not be designated to a 'Legacy Fund' with no intention as to its use.

- The separate identification of funds does not require them to be kept in separate bank accounts, but this may be a useful practice in some circumstances.
- In the past, many parishes have operated with a large number of funds for different aspects of the Church's life. Such a large number involves administrative complexity in the accounting system and the published financial statements. PCCs are recommended to keep under review the number of funds while taking care not to conflict with the strict rules on restricted and endowment funds. The PCC should consider:
  - closing the fund by using all the assets for the purpose for which it was set up;
  - identifying and reversing designated transfers the PCC may have made in the past, unless such money has been clearly spent or has a continuing purpose;
  - seeking assistance from the Charity Commission to modify the purpose for which the funds are held.
- PCCs are advised to ensure that they have proper systems in place for the signing of cheques, the counting of collections (including the opening of planned giving envelopes) and their prompt payment into the bank. Charity Commission leaflet CC8 provides useful information.

chapter 4

What money should the PCC account for?

4.1 This chapter should be read by every PCC to discover the responsibility that it has for the accounts of activities within the life of the Church or parish. That responsibility should have been clarified when this accounting framework came into force in 1997 but the information is repeated here for your attention.

Responsibility

4.2 It is clear that the PCC should account for its incoming resources and for the way those resources are expended, but in many parishes it is not easy to identify just what the PCC is responsible for.

4.3 One of the principles of the charity accounting regime is that trustees of a charity (PCC members) should identify and include in the annual financial statements any charitable funds that form part of it in law. The principal issue is how wide the net needs to be to meet the regime and also continue to satisfy local accountability to the Church electoral roll. Of course the wider the net is drawn the more likely larger PCCs are to move up into a higher income band but, if the net is not drawn widely enough, the PCC may fail to account for areas that are legally within its control.

4.4 The following are examples of situations that might arise. What are being described are entities that may be connected with the Church and whose funds may be under the control of the PCC:

- The PCC may have parochial organizations (such as a men's group, a young wives' group, a Boys' Brigade Company or a Church Hall Management Committee) that operate as a part of the local church and are not controlled by another body (such as the Mothers' Union or the Girl Guides). The members may pay contributions which are used to cover the cost of meetings, refreshments, duplicating and speakers' expenses. The organization may make a contribution to the PCC for the use of a meeting room or for the cost of heating and lighting.
- The PCC may also have funds that are administered by members of the congregation, such as a flower fund to cover the cost of flowers in church or a choir fund with some of the money received for weddings.
- There may also be a 'Friends' organization or other parochial trust to which parishioners are invited to contribute.
- There may also be various trusts, perhaps with the incumbent and churchwardens as trustees, and with the passage of time the control of the funds may have appeared to move to the PCC or the purpose of the funds may have become uncertain. (These may commonly be called 'Vicar and Wardens' trusts – see para. 4.17.)

4.5 It is important to remember that the purpose of PCC annual reports and financial statements is to make its financial activities transparent to those who read them. R&P accounts should show all that has been received and paid by the PCC or on its behalf; accruals accounts should include a Statement of Financial Activities (SOFA) that gives a true and fair view of all the financial activities of the PCC. This means that incoming resources that historically were not included in the PCC's financial statements may now need to be included on the basis that they do form part of its charitable funds.

4.6 The requirements of the accounting regime should be seen as an opportunity to bring back under the control of the PCC various extraneous groups which have gone off on their own.

Tests that should be applied

4.7 To discover whether the funds of a particular group should be included within the PCC's financial statements, the questions in the first box after para. 4.19 should be addressed. These will test whether the activity is a special trust of the PCC or otherwise under its control. It may be that the PCC needs to make a public declaration about its responsibilities for particular parochial groups, organizations and activities. It is recommended that the PCC annually reviews, for accounting purposes, the list of all organizations for which it wishes to take responsibility or may have to take responsibility.

Applying the tests in practice

4.8 The following are examples of conclusions drawn from applying the tests:

- Funds raised using the PCC's charitable status to reclaim tax must be included within the PCC's financial statements. This applies to activities, such as a Mission Gift Day, when the money will eventually be given away outside the parish.
- Monies collected by parochial activities, such as women's or men's groups that are not associated with a parent organization and are not under the control of the PCC, need not be included. However, each organization should be encouraged to account for its income to its members. If the PCC underwrites such activities (i.e. pays the bills if the organizers cannot) then they are within PCC control.
- Monies that are collected by parochial organizations that are associated with a parent organization, such as the Mothers' Union, are not included. These sums will be dealt with as a part of the financial statements of that organization and any contribution made to the PCC for the use of meeting rooms will be received and recorded by the PCC, probably as a donation or as income from the letting of facilities. The organizations may be noted in the financial statements as connected charities.
- Monies, usually restricted as to their use, that have historically been collected by members of the congregation for various purposes, such as the provision of church flowers. Usually these resources have been handled totally separately from the PCC accounts and the interest of the PCC treasurer is considered to be an intrusion. However they are, and should be accounted for as, restricted income of the PCC. It has to be recognized that this will be a sensitive issue in some parishes.
- A 'Friends' organization that raises funds for the upkeep of the church buildings. If the organization is a registered charity, it will account separately and make returns to the Charity Commission, but it will need to be mentioned in the PCC's financial statements as a connected charity. If it is treated as an excepted charity under the umbrella of the PCC, then it is a branch and its accounts should be included with the PCC's financial statements.

  A 'Friends' or other charitable organization that is not under the PCC's 'umbrella' and does not have its own charity registration may or may not be a problem. If it is for exclusively charitable purposes and has a gross income below the registration threshold (currently £5,000) it is not required to register with the Commission but it should have a constitution and must still prepare accounts and behave charitably. If its income is above the registration threshold then those managing it are in breach of charity law and should correct this by either registering as an autonomous charity or coming under the control of the PCC.

4.9 The PCC should not include in its own financial statements the income or expenditure of a registered charity connected with the Church (possibly the 'Friends') but the Charities SORP requires any material transactions between PCC and such connected charities to be disclosed. The 'Friends' should not settle PCC bills directly but should make a grant to the PCC, which will be accounted for as an incoming resource and as an appropriate expenditure.

4.10 A brief description of the basis on which income is recognized by the PCC should be included in the accounting policies.

What are trusts?

4.11 A trust is a device in English law to enable an appointed group of people to manage property and/or money for a specific purpose. The Trust Deed sets out how the trustees, of which there must normally be at least two, shall manage or dispense the assets of the trust. Not all trusts are charitable. To be charitable the trust must have a purpose that is charitable in law.

4.12 There may be a variety of charitable trusts within the parish. In order to account correctly for these it will be necessary to identify and classify them. This may require some work depending on how carefully they have been administered in the past (although it should only need to be done once). However, accounting requirements apart, it is important to ensure that property held on trust is administered by the right trustees and used for the right purpose.

4.13 There may be some trusts which are not part of or connected with the PCC and which will be subject to the normal registration and accounting regimes as with any other charity. These could include:

- The trust of a Church school site and associated endowments held by trustees other than the PCC (e.g. the incumbent and churchwardens).
- Other educational trusts not held by the PCC. Some parishes have Sunday school or religious education funds created by orders under section 2 of the Education Act 1973 (which has now become section 554 of the Education Act 1996). These 'three-fourteenths' trusts arise from the proceeds of sale of former Church school sites. It was traditional for the incumbent to have use of the school for half Saturday and all Sunday – hence three-fourteenths – and the Church school used the premises for the rest of the time. When the school is closed, three-fourteenths can remain in the parish, normally under the trusteeship of the incumbent and churchwardens (which was the traditional pattern for Church school trusteeship). The trust, if it has an income over £1,000, will have to be registered in its own right and accounted for under normal charity rules. It is not 'a hidden pot of gold' which can be appropriated for the PCC's general purposes.
- Other incumbent and churchwardens trusts will also be separate charities unless they are special trusts of the PCC (see paragraph 4.17).

4.14 Then there will be trusts which are or may be connected with the PCC. They may simply have to be accounted for as types of PCC fund, but it may be that they need to be 'tidied up' first, or that something can be done to make their administration more straightforward. Trusts in this category may be special trusts or subsidiary charities of the PCC. These are trusts of property held and administered by or on behalf of the PCC on separate trusts for any special purposes of the PCC:

- the property must be held on separate trusts (as could arise with a gift or legacy);
- it must be held and administered by or on behalf of the PCC, and so the trustees may not necessarily be the PCC itself;
- it must be held for a special purpose of the PCC and so a mere coincidence of objects is not sufficient – the trust must be for a purpose of the PCC.

4.15 Therefore a trust held by the incumbent and churchwardens for general ecclesiastical purposes in the parish would not be a special trust of the PCC even though the PCC could also use its general funds for these purposes, but a trust held by the incumbent and churchwardens for the express purpose of assisting the PCC in the maintenance of the churchyard would be a special trust of the PCC.

4.16 Sometimes, after carrying out all reasonable investigations, it will prove difficult or impossible to classify a particular trust or fund. If the amount involved is large it may be necessary to involve professional advisers to get to the bottom of the trust. However, if the amount is small so that the cost of unravelling the trust would be out of proportion to its assets, parishes may wish to adopt a common sense approach and account for the trust as a special trust of the PCC or a related charity so that at least it is accounted for somewhere.

Incumbent and churchwardens' trusts

4.17 Trusts where the incumbent and churchwardens are trustees generally fall into three categories:

Trusts for ecclesiastical purposes

(e.g. maintenance of the church and churchyard): these are already required to be vested in the Diocesan Board of Finance (DBF) as custodian trustee. They will have similar objects to those of the PCC.

Trusts for educational purposes

(e.g. Sunday school funds arising from the sale of a Church school): these are registered with the Department for Education. They are entirely separate from the PCC's financial statements, however there may be cases where it is helpful to note the existence of such charities for the information of parishioners.

Trusts for the relief of poverty

(e.g. to provide food or clothing for poor people in the parish): unless they are very small and have no permanent endowment, these should already be registered with the Charity Commission. Again, they are entirely separate from the PCC's financial statements, however there may be cases where it is helpful to note the existence of such charities for the information of parishioners.

4.18 Incumbent and churchwardens' trusts for ecclesiastical purposes may need to be shown as a part of the PCC's financial statements or they may need to be referred to in a note to the financial statements. The following situations will probably apply:

- Any trust that is being administered by the PCC must be accounted for by the PCC. If the objects are narrower than the objects of the PCC, it will be a restricted fund.
- A trust that is administered separately by the incumbent and churchwardens may be referred to in a note to the financial statements.
- Where another charity pays for items which would normally form part of the PCC's expenditure, then the expenditure from the trust must be shown as part of the PCC's income, by means of a grant to the PCC, and the relevant expenditure shown as PCC expenditure.

4.19 It should be noted that incumbents and churchwardens, as trustees of these trusts, have a responsibility to account and any member of the public can ask for a copy of the financial statements of such trusts.

Is the PCC responsible? Questions to ask

Question 1

Is this group so constituted that it is in law a special trust of the PCC? (A special trust in section 97 of the Charities Act 1993 is defined as 'property which is held and administered by or on behalf of a charity for any special purposes of the charity, and is so held and administered on separate trusts relating only to that property').

- If it is a special trust, whoever is controlling it is accountable to the PCC and the PCC must include it in its financial statements. It will be a restricted fund of the PCC. (See paras 4.11 to 4.19 for more information.)
- If not, go to the next question.

Question 2

Does the PCC control the group? Related questions that may help to tease out the relationship relate to whether the group has a separate constitution; whether it recognizes the authority of the PCC; whether the group is a separate charitable institution. Using the Church's name and registration with HMRC for reclaiming tax brings it under the PCC's control but just using the Church's name in the group's title does not.

- If it is controlled by the PCC, it is a part of the PCC, in which case it should follow the requirements of the PCC in keeping records.
- If it is not under the control of the PCC, it may be an autonomous group and, if it is for exclusively charitable purposes, it is accountable in law and has all the responsibilities and costs of running a charity, but go to Question 3.

Question 3

Is the group under the control of some of the members of the PCC and are they acting as a subcommittee of the PCC in their control? If the PCC members outnumber the others in the control of the group, then it is under the control of the PCC. The incumbent acting as a member of the PCC under its delegation may fulfil this function. For example, if the incumbent can remove officers of the Boys' Brigade or restructure the control of the unit, it is then appropriate to ask whether the incumbent is acting in his/her own right or on behalf of the PCC. (It should be noted that the incumbent may be three bodies: acting in his/her own right as a person; acting solely as a corporation; or acting as chair of the PCC.)

- If yes, then it has been established that the group is not under the control of the full PCC. There appear to be some PCC members involved in controlling the group – are they acting as a delegated committee?
- If yes, then you are back to the answer to Question 2.
- If no, then the question must be asked whether both sides think it is a connected charity – it is going to be connected by having parallel, common or related objects and being administered by common administration or common trustees.

Tips for identifying trusts

- It is important to find the governing instrument for the trust. This may be a conveyance of land, a separate trust deed, a constitution, a Charity Commission scheme, a Will or even a resolution or letter.
- The papers or copies of them should be held locally, but papers are often lost or mislaid as the personalities involved change. The diocesan office may have them, but don't expect the diocesan secretary to do the research for you. Diocesan secretaries will be receiving similar requests from dozens of other parishes and will not have the time to act as trust adviser to them all. Ask instead if you can inspect the trust papers which the diocese is holding for your parish.
- The Charity Commission may have information, particularly if the charity is registered or it has a file on it for any other reason. The Commission register is available on the internet.
- Local records offices and archivists or the National Archives may have copies of deeds and other important documents.
- If sufficient details are known, copies of Wills can be obtained from the Probate Service.

Tips for tidying up trusts

- You may find that a trust has no properly appointed trustees and appointments have to be made.
- If it is impossible to appoint trustees (perhaps because the governing document provided for the original trustees to appoint their own successors and they died without doing so) the Charity Commission can make an order to appoint some.
- The objects of the trust may now be obsolete or outdated, or they may be so similar to the objects of the PCC itself that it would be sensible to transfer the trust assets to the PCC. Consider obtaining a scheme from the Charity Commission or taking advantage of the small charities provisions in section 74 of the Charities Act 1993 (the Charity Commission produces leaflets on these topics).
- The trust may have a permanent endowment in the form of investments which produce an income so small that it is of no use to anyone. Section 75 of the Charities Act 1993 provides a means by which these very small charities can spend their capital. Again, the Charity Commission can provide leaflets and information.
- If the trust's assets are very small and are not a permanent endowment, it may be sensible to spend them all on some purpose within the objects of the trust and the trust will then come to an end.

Tips for handling other church funds

- The treasurer (on behalf of the PCC) should ensure that proper accounting records are kept by PCC 'branches' (organizations and those who hold the purses for small extra funds for which the PCC is accountable in law). Each year the treasurer will need to obtain an accurate return from each 'branch', which can be quite simple, consisting of a summary of Receipts and Payments for the year, and a list of any assets and liabilities at the year-end. The figures from these organizations or funds should be added to the PCC's financial statements if they are material.
- Unless these 'branches' are a separately accountable legal entity, all the funds that they hold are the legal property of the PCC, whether or not they have a separate bank account.
- 'Friends' organizations not under the control of the PCC should be advised to have themselves properly constituted.
- There are other important reasons for establishing the status of Church organizations, such as concerns over insurance cover and responsibilities under the Children Act 1989.
- Fees are earned by the incumbent and also by the PCC. These are separate fees: one forms part of the PCC's income whilst the other is the incumbent's income. Often, an incumbent will assign his/her fees to the diocese. If the fees are not assigned, they will have to be declared and the incumbent's stipend is reduced accordingly. It is therefore important that, when one cheque is received for both types of fee, the treasurer ensures that the relevant portion is paid to the incumbent. The treasurer should not include the incumbent's fee as part of PCC income in any way because he is only acting as an agent for the incumbent if he collects fees on the incumbent's behalf.

chapter 5

Assets and their valuation

5.1 This chapter should be read by those PCCs who either choose to or who have to prepare their financial statements on the accruals accounting basis. It describes how assets should be accounted for. PCCs using the R&P accounting basis may wish to refer to the summary box and the description of assets at the end of this chapter may also be of interest.

Accountability

5.2 In order to account correctly for assets, PCCs need to understand what funds they hold in trust, what funds are held on their behalf for which they are responsible, and how they should value the assets of all these funds according to their use. In general terms, assets for which PCCs are responsible fall into the following groups for accounting purposes:

(i) intangible assets such as purchased goodwill or copyright royalties (rare in practice);

(ii) tangible fixed assets used for the work of the PCC;

(iii) consecrated and benefice property;

(iv) assets held for investment purposes;

(v) other (current) assets.

5.3 Each of these groups of assets may have different valuation rules. For PCCs preparing receipts and payment accounts the assets owned by the PCC need only be listed in the Statement of Assets and Liabilities. PCCs preparing accruals accounts will need to refer to the following paragraphs.

5.4 The Church of England has complex rules about ownership of assets. PCCs may be trustees of income and expenditure relating to assets of which they are not the legal owner and in relation to which they are not accountable under Part VI of the Charities Act 1993. Most PCCs will be in the following position with regard to their tangible fixed assets (items ii and iii as listed above):

- They have maintenance responsibility for the consecrated land/buildings and certain other (benefice) properties within the parish. The Charities Act 1993 states in section 96(2) that benefice property (sub-section (a)) and consecrated property (sub-section (c)) are removed from the definition of charity for the purposes of the Act. Therefore these assets should not be included in the financial statements though they may be referred to in the notes. Costs associated with the maintenance or improvement of such assets will be written off in the year they are incurred.

- They have responsibility for ensuring that the buildings are adequately insured and it is recommended, though not mandatory, that the insurance valuation of the buildings is included in a note to the financial statements for reference.

- The various items of movable church furnishings are vested in churchwardens for the use and benefit of the parishioners and cannot be disposed of without a faculty. These assets are regarded as 'inalienable' property held on special trust on behalf of the PCC, and should not be accounted for in the PCC's accounts. Expenditure to renew, improve or add to them should be written off as an expense in the financial year in which it occurs.

- As benefice property, the parsonage house is excluded from accountability by section 96(2)(a) of the Charities Act 1993 and therefore should not be included in the financial statements.

- They have other buildings e.g. church halls, curates' houses etc. The titles of these are likely to be held by a diocesan body on behalf of the parish. As fixed assets of the PCC that are held for continuing use in its work, these should all be included in the balance sheet at either their cost or a trustees valuation. As functional assets (not investment assets) they do not have to be shown at market value. When brought into the balance sheet for the first time the valuation should be given. If the asset was a gift, then the value at the date of the gift should be used. All such assets should be depreciated accordingly.

- They have 'functional equipment' that is used on a continuing basis for the work of the PCC. Examples include: office equipment (computers etc), ground and building maintenance equipment and vehicles. These are fixed assets and (apart from any immaterial items which have been treated as an expense) should be included in the balance sheet – this will normally be at cost less depreciation.

5.5 In law 'consecration' is not considered to be the same as 'dedication' as the latter is no more than an expression of pious intention that the building or land is given back to God. By act of consecration, property is effectively dedicated to God and set aside solely for sacred purposes.

5.6 The methods and principles on which assets are to be included in the balance sheet are included in the model set of accounting policies at the end of Chapter 8.

5.7 Great care should be taken using the insured value for balance sheet valuation purposes, unless the insurance is for only the fair value of the asset taking into account its existing condition (i.e. 'total loss' replacement cost less a deduction for wear and tear to date). The value in a 'replacement as new' policy would need to be modified accordingly to bring it to a fair value.

Accounting for fixed assets

5.8 Subject to paragraph 5.12, all assets (including inalienable assets) which are unconsecrated, i.e. not encompassed by section 96(2)(a) of the Charities Act 1993, should be capitalized and disclosed in the relevant balance sheet categories and related notes. For example:

(a) An investment property should be included as an investment within fixed assets, valued at open market value and disclosed within the investment notes as part of investment properties.

(b) Functional properties used by a PCC in undertaking its activities, for example the church hall and offices, should be included within tangible fixed assets. They should be carried at cost, or at a reasonable estimate of the asset's cost or current value to the charity, less depreciation. Regular revaluation is not necessary, however if a valuation policy is adopted, under FRS 15, revaluations should be every five years with an interim review in the third year. Revaluations may be undertaken by suitably qualified trustees or employees.

(c) Tangible fixed assets other than unconsecrated properties (e.g. movable church furnishings that cannot be disposed of without a faculty) should be included at cost or valued at open market value.

Where assets are capitalized under (b) or (c) above, several years after being acquired, they should be included at original cost or at their estimated value when acquired by the PCC if they were donated. However, if neither of these amounts is ascertainable, a reasonable estimate of the asset's current cost or value to the PCC may be used. Such a valuation will be regarded as the asset's initial carrying amount and will not be regarded as a revaluation. These assets will need to be depreciated over their estimated useful lives in accordance with a disclosed policy, or alternatively be subject to an annual impairment review. A policy of non-depreciation can only be adopted if both the annual depreciation charge and the accumulated depreciation is not material to the financial statements as the assets have a very long remaining useful life, or the residual value (in the case of freehold property this would normally be the value of the land) is higher than the cost or value at which they are included in the financial statements.

5.9 FRS 15 requires that all fixed assets should be capitalized in the balance sheet. In principle this includes fixed assets that are inalienable and heritage assets, such as heritage buildings.

5.10 An 'inalienable asset' is one which a charity is required by law to retain indefinitely for its own use/benefit and therefore cannot dispose of without external consent. This includes assets that cannot be sold without a faculty as they are held on trust, which contemplates their retention and continuing use and not disposal. However, it does not include consecrated or benefice property for which PCCs are responsible.

5.11 'Heritage assets' are defined as assets of historical or artistic importance that are held to advance preservation, conservation and educational objectives of charities and, through public access, contribute to the nation's culture and education at either national or local level. Such assets are central to the achievement of the purposes of such charities and include the land, buildings, structures, collections, exhibits or artefacts that are preserved or conserved and are central to the educational objectives of such charities. The primary objective of any PCC is not the preservation of the buildings they occupy or the furnishings and other artefacts for which they are responsible and therefore none of a PCC's assets will be heritage assets, even though some may be of considerable historical or artistic importance.

5.12 A number of PCCs have assets, e.g. historic buildings and artefacts contained in the church, that would be heritage assets if the PCC had preservation or conservation objects. Such assets are used by the church, for example for worship, but valuing them when they have not been previously included in accounts in order to follow FRS15 principles might be impractical. This is because reliable cost information is not available and conventional valuation approaches (such as using the current cost of construction) lack sufficient reliability. In such cases they should not be valued in the accounts but the notes should contain a statement to that effect, explaining the reasons why. The notes should also contain information that enables the reader to appreciate the age, scale and nature of the excluded assets and the use made of them.

CATEGORY	R&P ACCOUNTS NO VALUATIONS	ACCRUALS ACCOUNTS	
		RECOGNITION	VALUATION
Consecrated land and buildings and other property Parsonage house	Not included in accounts May note existence in TAR	Not included in accounts May note existence in TAR	No valuation required
Movable church furnishings	Not included in accounts May note existence in TAR	Not included in accounts May note existence in TAR	No valuation required
Other functional assets (e.g. curate's house, church hall, equipment)	Note details in Statement of Assets and Liabilities	Include	Cost or valuation in use, less depreciation
Investment assets	Note details in Statement of Assets and Liabilities	Include	Market value
Current assets (except those that are investments)	Note details in Statement of Assets and Liabilities	Include	Lower of cost or realizable value
Liabilities	Note details in Statement of Assets and Liabilities	Include	The value at which the liability will be settled

chapter 6

Analysis of incoming resources and resources expended

6.1 This chapter should be read by all PCCs as it lists the various incoming resources and items of expenditure for which PCCs may be responsible and collates them under headings which are statutory for PCCs which are over the audit threshold.

Analysis

6.2 PCCs that are over the audit threshold must prepare their financial statements on the accruals basis, and must analyse their incoming and expended resources under certain specific headings. SORP 2005 requires charities to structure their Statement of Financial Activities in such a way as to identify the main elements of incoming resources and resources expended based on activities. PCCs under the audit threshold preparing accruals accounts are not required to do this but are encouraged to do so as a matter of good practice. These smaller PCCs may instead choose resource categories appropriate to their circumstances.

6.3 This list is given *as an aid and all items need not be separately included in the financial statements.* The principle of materiality will decide which to show separately.

6.4 While smaller PCCs and those who choose to adopt R&P accounts do not have to follow these activity headings, it is strongly recommended that they do so. This will make it easier for those who wish to compare PCC accounts and for the completion of annual Returns of Parish Finance to the diocese or Archbishops' Council.

6.5 The headings given in **bold** type are those that correspond to the SORP 2005 requirements. The examples of items to be included under each heading should be disclosed in the notes to the financial statements unless immaterial.

Incoming resources

6.6 All resources which become available to a PCC and which must be applied in furtherance of its charitable purposes should be included. Some of the sub-categories are based on the grouping of information required by the Return of Parish Finance.

Incoming resources from generated funds

Voluntary income

Planned giving:

Money given either in envelopes or through a bankers' order or by cheque.

Income tax recoverable on planned giving:
This must be shown separately and, if no tax recovery claim has been made, an explanation should be given in a note to the financial statements. Note: Income tax recoverable on other voluntary income should be shown under that particular sub-category (e.g. Sundry donations).

Other giving:
Money given in envelopes without a declaration, one-off gifts by Gift Aid and money given through Charities Aid Foundation (or other) vouchers or through Payroll Giving (Give As You Earn).

Collections (other than planned giving through envelopes):
At all services to be used for ordinary purposes.
Restricted collections for missions and charities.
Sunday school collection.

Gift days.

Sundry donations:
Given by individuals for ordinary purposes.
Given through church boxes and wall safes.

Grants:
These may be restricted funds from the Local Authority for upkeep to the churchyard, from English Heritage for the building, from the diocese towards stipends or from a local trust fund.

Donations, appeals, etc. (including for restricted purposes).

Gifts of quoted securities (accruals accounts only).

Legacies:
These should be included in the financial statements as soon as they are legally enforceable and capable of financial measurement (R&P accounts: when received).

Donated services and facilities:
The quantified value of donated assistance that the PCC would otherwise have had to purchase (accruals accounts only).

Activities for generating funds

Bookstall:
Money received from the sale of books, periodicals and stationery for the purposes of fund-raising.

Church hall lettings, etc. for non-church purposes:
Include income from letting church to non-church users.

Rummage sales, fetes, bazaars and other fund-raising events where goods sold have been donated to the church:
The income must be stated gross, unless the expenses of running the fund-raising activity were immaterial. The money may have been raised for the unrestricted general fund or for restricted purposes.

The generation of funds through any other business activities primarily undertaken for that purpose rather than as forming part of the work of the church. This includes fund-raising where PCC funds were not put at risk (such as use of a Webb Ivory catalogue).

Investment income

Dividends.

Bank and Building Society interest including any reclaimed tax on investment income
(interest arising from restricted funds must be allocated to those funds).

Rent from land or other buildings owned by PCC for investment purposes.

Incoming resources from charitable activities

Bookstall:
Money received from the sale of books, periodicals and stationery for the purposes of promoting the church's objects (see 8.51).

Church hall lettings, etc. for purposes within the objects of the PCC:
Include income from the use of the church hall and other church buildings.

Parish magazines:
The income through sales.

Fees paid to the PCC for weddings, funerals, training courses, etc.

Other incoming resources

Insurance claims (Receipts & Payments only):

Insurance claims are indemnity payments and may be netted off against expenditure to the extent that they do not include a profit or gain element (e.g. 'new for old'). Where the insurer pays a supplier's bill direct (as is often the case with vehicle damage claims) that amount should not be shown as a payment and receipt.

Surplus on sale of fixed assets:

This is the sale proceeds less the net book value at the date of sale. (In R&P accounts this will be the sale proceeds without deduction.)

Resources expended

6.7 All expenditure in all the PCC's funds should be included here and expenditure related to each activity group should be disclosed in the Statement of Financial Activities, where material, or the notes to the financial statements. All expenditure should be recognized as it is incurred but, for accruals accounts, commitments which are regarded as constructive obligations should be included.

Include items that correspond to gifts in kind and donated services and facilities where appropriate in accruals accounts.

Costs of generating funds

Costs of generating voluntary income

Fees paid to a professional fund raiser.

Costs incurred in applying for grants or donations.

Costs of a Christian Stewardship campaign:

(including printing, postage, supply of materials, speakers' expenses, costs levied by the diocese for the services of a Stewardship adviser). Cost of stewardship giving envelopes.

Fund-raising trading: cost of goods sold and other costs

Bookstall cost of goods sold for fund-raising purposes and associated running costs.

Cost of fêtes, bazaars, other fund-raising events:

(including the cost of the provision of materials, advertising, hire of equipment, hire of venue).

Investment management costs

Any investment management costs (The PCC is required to take professional advice on the selection of investments).

Charitable activities

Grants made in furtherance of the PCC's objectives:

Missionary and charitable giving

Church overseas

(including payments to the recognized missionary societies (CMS, USPG, etc.), other overseas missions and diocesan associations and missionary councils).

Relief and development agencies

(including payments to Christian Aid, TEAR Fund and similar Christian organizations concerned primarily with relief and development aid agencies).

Home missions and other Church societies and organizations
(include payments to Church Army, Children's Society, Mothers' Union, Church Urban Fund and similar organizations).

Secular charities
(include payments to Oxfam, Help the Aged, Save the Children Fund and other charities which are secularly based).

Ministry:

Diocesan quota/Parish Share/Family Purse
(when dioceses break down this figure into smaller constituent parts, such as ministry, diocesan support and insurance, these parts may be shown elsewhere under the relevant heading).

Working expenses of incumbent:
Telephone, postage, stationery, car/public transport, secretarial assistance, office equipment, maintenance of robes, hospitality, provision of locum tenens and visiting speakers.

Parsonage house
Repairs, water rates, interior redecoration.

Assistant staff (mainly as for incumbent)
Assistant clergy

Pastoral staff

Youth workers

(including expenses of visiting clergy and speakers).

Church – running expenses
Heating, lighting, cleaning, insurance.

Church maintenance
Minor repairs including routine maintenance, organ/piano tuning.

Upkeep of services
Altar requisites, repair and replacement of service books, music, leaflets, choir robes.

Upkeep of churchyard
Care of church grounds, routine maintenance including wages and contracts, repair of mower and other equipment, grass cutting.

Expenditure on parish magazine, bookstall
Cost of books and other materials.
Printing costs for the magazine and other editorial costs.

Training costs
Parish training and mission.
Education (Church day school, Sunday school, lay training and other educational expenses).

Hall running costs
Water rates, routine maintenance and repair, insurance premium, heating, lighting, cleaning equipment, wages of the cleaner.

Other PCC property upkeep
Various items as for hall.

Major repairs (structure).

Major repairs/replacements (installations).

Interior and exterior redecoration.

Salaries/wages/honoraria (and National Insurance where applicable)
Verger, clerk, sexton, organist, choir
(these should be split as necessary to reflect the functional purpose).

Movable furnishings and equipment:

Depreciation (accounts on the accruals basis only).

Costs of additions/renewals (accounts on the R&P basis only).

New building or major works
Church.

Larger parishes may wish to consider reporting their Charitable Expenditure in categories which are commensurate with their objectives and activities set out in the Annual Report (see 9.27).

Governance costs

Governance costs include the costs of governance arrangements which relate to the general running of the PCC as opposed to the direct management functions inherent in generating funds and the work of the parish. Governance activities provide the governance infrastructure which allows the PCC to operate and to generate the information required for public accountability. The costs will normally include internal and external audit; legal advice for PCC members; and costs associated with constitutional and statutory requirements, e.g. the cost of PCC meetings and preparing annual reports and accounts. Included within this category are any costs associated with the strategic as opposed to day-to-day management of the PCC's activities.

Other resources expended

Any expenditure which does not fall within the main resources expended categories. This should not be used for support costs, which can be allocated to other activity costs.

Support costs

When resources expended are analysed by activity, there are some costs which cannot be allocated directly to activities because they support more than one activity. Such support costs are costs that are necessary to deliver an activity but do not themselves produce or constitute the output of the activity. They may include central costs such as the parish office, and a certain proportion of clergy time and the costs of buildings and equipment.

By their nature, support costs can seldom be allocated directly to activities and therefore they must be apportioned between a number of activities. When a PCC is over the audit threshold, it must classify its expenditure according to the three main activities: fund raising, church (charitable) activities and governance and in this situation it must apportion any support costs between these activities. However a PCC below the audit threshold is not required to do this and there is no need to apportion support costs.

If support costs are separately identified and apportioned the basis for doing this should be reported in the notes to the accounts.

chapter 7

Accounts on the Receipts & Payments basis

7.1 This chapter contains guidance for PCCs preparing a Receipts & Payments account and Statement of Assets and Liabilities (the R&P basis). PCCs who either choose to or are required to prepare accounts on the accruals basis should read Chapter 8 instead.

7.2 Guidance on which PCCs may prepare accounts on the R&P basis is included in Chapter 1.

Introduction

7.3 PCCs below the accruals accounts threshold may adopt the R&P basis for financial statements in order to minimize the burden in preparing accounts. In many cases parishes may find that the approach they have adopted in the past can continue, with the addition of the statutory Statement of Assets and Liabilities and the written Annual Report. The practices set out in this chapter are only recommendations and are not mandatory.

7.4 The financial statements should not describe items as either 'income' or 'expenditure' since that may suggest that the accruals basis of accounts has been adopted. A 'half-way house' – part accruals and part R&P – is not allowed by law. The Statement of Assets and Liabilities must never be called a 'balance sheet', nor should it be 'balanced' since this too may suggest that the accruals basis of accounts has been adopted.

7.5 In preparing the financial statements, PCCs should bear in mind that these form part of their accountability to members of the church as well as to the public and therefore the financial statements should, as far as possible, communicate a clear picture. They should be approved at a meeting of the PCC and signed. The Regulations only require one signature, that of the chairman of the meeting. However, in the case of the Church of England, where the chairman of the meeting will normally be the minister, it is good practice for the financial statements also to be signed by one other member, normally the treasurer or churchwarden, to underline the joint responsibility of both the minister and the laity of the PCC.

7.6 Practical examples are included in Chapter 14 and it may be helpful to follow these when reading this chapter.

General principles

Disclosure of accounting basis

7.7 The R&P account for the year is a factual summary of money received and paid during the financial year. A Statement of Assets and Liabilities is a list of significant possessions and outstanding financial obligations as at the end of the year. Because the R&P account and Statement of Assets and Liabilities differ from other forms of annual financial statements in important ways (for example by not including 'prepayments' and 'accruals', and not recording the increase or decrease in total funds caused by valuations of assets), the financial statements should include a clear statement that they have been prepared on the 'R&P basis'.

7.8 The fundamental accounting principle that must be applied in the preparation of R&P accounts concerns the issue of consistency. However, the materiality principle should also be considered in the preparation of such accounts.

Consistency

7.9 The annual financial statements should be 'consistent'. This means that items of the same kind are shown in the financial statements in the same way and the year-to-year treatment is the same.

Materiality

7.10 Only items which are 'material' to the view given by the financial statements should be shown by the PCC separately in its financial statements or described in its annual report. A definition of materiality is provided in the Glossary of terms in Chapter 12. For R&P accounts the materiality principle relates to the separate disclosure of items rather than to their inclusion within the financial statements.

Accounting for different types of fund

7.11 As explained in Chapter 3 a PCC may have unrestricted and restricted income and endowment funds available to it. Unrestricted funds are those held for spending on the general purposes of the PCC and may be designated for specific purposes.

7.12 Where a PCC holds both restricted and unrestricted funds, they must be distinguished either by preparing a separate R&P account for each fund or by grouping the funds in a combined account and sub-analysing them by way of note. Similarly, the fund group to which each asset and liability belongs should be shown in the year-end statement of assets and liabilities. If this is not done, it appears to the reader of the financial statements that all funds are held on exactly the same basis and may increase the risk that the PCC will begin to ignore fund restrictions. This must be avoided, since to spend restricted funds outside the terms of the restriction is a breach of trust.

7.13 As indicated in Chapter 3 R&P accounts may be prepared in a columnar format in order to disclose each fund separately. If this approach is adopted a comparative column for the previous year does not have to show the split of all funds and can just be the total of all restricted and unrestricted fund R&P.

The Receipts & Payments account

7.14 The R&P account is a simple statement of account which summarizes cash (including cash equivalents e.g. bank and building society balances (except term deposits)) transactions in the period. It is a form of account that is used by many smaller PCCs and is easily understood. A definition of the term 'Receipts & Payments account' is provided in the Glossary of terms. A receipt should be taken into account when cash or a cheque is physically received by the PCC, not only when the cheque clears through its bank account. Payments should be taken into account when cash is physically handed over by the PCC or when a cheque is written and released. Transfers into and out of deposit accounts requiring notice for withdrawal and which are shown separately from cash and bank balances in the statement of assets and liabilities should also be accounted for.

Receipts

7.15 All amounts received of the same type should be added together and the totals should be shown under appropriate headings in the financial statements. Some appropriate headings are provided in Chapter 6. The corresponding figures for the previous financial year should be given for each item in the list of receipts, for comparison.

Planned giving, collections, donations, gifts, legacies and grants

7.16 All cash receipts from planned giving, collections, donations, gifts, legacies, grants and other voluntary sources should be included in the R&P account on the date the cash is actually received.

7.17 A donation, gift, legacy or other receipt which is received in the form of assets (see Glossary) other than cash cannot be shown in the R&P account until the PCC converts it into cash by selling it. In that event, the cash receipt should be entered in the financial statements at the time the property is sold and the money received.

7.18 If the asset has not been sold by the end of the year and still belongs to the PCC, it should be included in the Statement of Assets and Liabilities with a note of the fund of which it forms part. If the asset is sold for cash in the following year, the cash receipt should be shown in the following year's R&P account.

7.19 Sometimes a PCC receives a donation or gift in a form other than cash, which (rather than being sold) is distributed in the form in which it was received. Gifts of clothing, for example, may be immediately passed on to beneficiaries as a means of charitable provision. In these circumstances the PCC neither receives nor pays out cash, so nothing is able to be shown in the R&P account. If the gift is material, its receipt and subsequent distribution should be described in the annual report.

Other benefits received by the PCC

7.20 A PCC may receive a benefit in a form other than money or other assets. For instance, someone may make an interest-free loan to the PCC or may offer to perform some service (such as an aspect of maintenance of the church) without charge. Benefits of this latter sort are known as donated services and facilities and cannot be shown in a R&P account since the benefit is non-monetary. Instead, the benefit, if material, should be described in the annual report in a way which properly illustrates its value and importance to the PCC.

Trading Receipts & Payments

7.21 Any receipts from trading should be shown gross in the R&P account. It is not acceptable simply to show the profit received from the trading. This means, for example, that the total proceeds of the sale of parish magazines must be shown as receipts, and the costs of printing the magazine should be shown as payments. In the case of a fund-raising event, the proceeds of the event should be shown as receipts, with the costs of organizing the event shown as payments. If the event has been organized by a separately accountable body outside the PCC and the proceeds donated to the Church, they should be shown net as a donation.

7.22 This treatment applies to any form of trading, whether directly connected with the PCC's purposes (the sale of religious books on the church bookstall, for instance) or whether carried out purely in order to raise funds. It applies where the trading is regular or permanent and where it is occasional. The only exception to this is where the event or activity concerned is small scale and so the receipts and payments involved are not material in the context of the overall transactions of the PCC.

7.23 Examples of fund-raising trading carried out by PCCs include Christmas card sales, fetes, bazaars, missionary lunches, garden parties and other fund-raising events, and the letting of church premises, rent from land or buildings where this is not for church purposes. Examples of charitable trading include: Alpha courses, bookstall and letting of buildings for church purposes. When reporting trading income, trading for charitable purposes should always be separated from trading for Church fund-raising purposes.

Recovery of tax

7.24 The PCC will receive Gift Aid donations where the tax is recovered from HMRC separately from the donations. Tax recovered in this way should be shown as a separate receipt from the income on which the tax was recovered. If a PCC receives interest or other income from investments net of tax (that is, tax has been deducted from the income before it was passed to the PCC), the PCC will have to recover the tax separately later.

7.25 If the PCC is entitled to recover tax and has not received it before its financial year-end, it cannot yet be shown as a receipt in the R&P account. Instead, the amount of tax re-claimable should be noted as an asset in the Statement of Assets and Liabilities with the explanation that it has not yet been received. When the tax refund is received it should then be shown in the R&P account.

7.26 Many PCCs make a single tax claim in relation to the tax year (April to March), but more frequent claims are encouraged by HMRC. If there are significant arrears in tax recovered, reference should be made to the future recovery of tax in the statement of assets and liabilities and in the PCC's annual report since the PCC has a responsibility to recover the tax on tax-efficient contributions.

Receipts from charitable activities

7.27 This should include any receipts that the PCC has generated from its work including PCC fees for services (weddings and funerals), letting of church property for church purposes, membership subscriptions from various groups (e.g. youth, parents and toddlers), bookstall and magazine receipts (but any advertising revenue may be best shown as donations).

Investment receipts

7.28 This will include any interest and dividends received from investments and the letting of any investment property.

Other receipts

7.29 Other receipts will include any monies received from insurance claims made by the PCC. These should be included in the R&P account when received. If at 31 December insurers have agreed the claim and the amount to be paid, this should be shown in the Statement of Assets and Liabilities as a debtor under the monetary assets category. It should also include money from the sale of investment or fixed assets. Neither of these will normally count towards gross income (see also paragraph 2.9).

Payments

7.30 It is likely that the most critical issue is to ensure that payments are properly classified into the recommended categories as detailed in Chapter 6. It is, therefore, important that the PCC's accounting records are set up in a manner which enables the easy analysis of payments in these classifications. The corresponding figures for the previous financial year should be given for each total, for comparison.

7.31 Where the PCC is aware of payments that are due to be paid at the year-end, such as outstanding diocesan parish share or independent examiner's fees, these should not be recorded in the R&P account until they are paid. Instead they should be noted as monetary liabilities in the Statement of Assets and Liabilities.

The Statement of Assets and Liabilities

Cash and bank deposits, including the CBF Church of England Deposit Fund

7.32 These are the cash resources of the PCC which are immediately available to it, and they should be listed as the first item in the Statement of Assets and Liabilities. A separate figure should be shown for the unrestricted funds and the total of the PCC's restricted funds. Deposits which must be left for a fixed period should not be included here, since the PCC does not have immediate access to the cash, but they should be included in the list of investments described in para. 7.36 below.

Other monetary assets

7.33 All debts and money owed to the PCC should be listed under this heading. This includes sums owed to the PCC as repayments (capital and interest) for loans made by it and tax recovery claims not yet received (see paras 7.24 to 7.26). Small sums of the same sort (for instance, parish magazine receipts due but not received) should be added together as one item.

7.34 A note should be added to each item to show the fund to which the item belongs.

7.35 Occasionally PCCs are told that they have been left something in a Will, but that it will be some time before they actually receive the cash or property comprising the legacy. If, at the end of the financial year, the PCC has not yet received the legacy but formal notification of the entitlement and amount has been received, particulars of it should be noted in the Statement of Assets and Liabilities.

Investment assets

7.36 Occasionally a PCC may hold an asset as an investment either to produce income or for capital growth or both. If so, it should be shown as an investment asset. This includes stocks and shares, cash deposits which must be left for a fixed term, common investment fund holdings, land with or without buildings, and interests in land such as a rent charge. If the PCC has set up a non-charitable trading company, any shares which the PCC owns in that company should also be included.

7.37 The list should show to which of the PCC's restricted or unrestricted funds the asset belongs. Its value (if known) at the year-end might be shown in a note but there is no need to provide valuations in a

Statement of Assets and Liabilities. However, the PCC needs to be aware of the approximate market value of any substantial investment assets to ensure it discharges its trustee responsibilities.

7.38 Where the investment asset is land (with or without buildings) the note should include the address and a brief description of the property (for example, 'subject to tenancy and currently used for short term letting'). It would also be helpful briefly to describe the age and condition of any buildings (for example, 'a three storey terraced house built around 1880 and in good structural and decorative repair').

Fixed assets used by the PCC

7.39 Assets held by the PCC mainly for its own use (rather than as investments) should be listed separately. Apart from church furnishings, which can be listed simply as 'inventory assets vested in the churchwardens on special trust', the most common assets of this sort will be land and buildings, but the category may also include motor vehicles, lawn mowers and office equipment (such as a computer) used for parish administration.

7.40 Assets of this sort should be included in the list whether they are owned outright or on hire-purchase terms. Assets that are leased will not be included where the ownership of the asset reverts to the lessor at the end of the lease.

Liabilities

7.41 A liability is a debt or obligation owed by the PCC, or a sum of money which the PCC is committed to paying at some time after the end of the present financial year. However, a commitment to pay a sum of money in future in return for a future benefit should not be treated as a liability. For example, an obligation to pay for goods already supplied to the PCC is a liability until the obligation is settled. But the obligation to make future rental payments under the terms of a lease of the PCC's photocopier should not be included as present liabilities, since full value in return for the future payments will be received in the same future accounting periods. Instead, the extent of the obligation should be noted (e.g. 'the PCC is committed to paying rent of £500 p.a. for a further 12 months under the existing hire agreement for the photocopier in the parish office').

7.42 Liabilities of different types should be listed separately, though several liabilities of the same type (for instance, small amounts owing to various suppliers) may be added together and shown as a single figure. An example of this is where bills may be outstanding for the gas and electrical supplies to the PCC.

7.43 The PCC should show, in a note, to which of its restricted or unrestricted funds each liability relates.

7.44 Examples of liabilities include any loans or overdrafts advanced to the PCC, any arrears of diocesan quota or parish share, monies held on behalf of third parties (for example, where a collection has been made for a missionary society) and creditors for goods and services. Any other potential liability not included in accordance with paragraphs 7.41 and 7.42, but which the PCC thinks likely to become payable at some time in the future on the occurrence or non-occurrence of an event should also be included in the Statement of Assets and Liabilities, together with a note explaining how and why the liability arises.

Notes to the financial statements

7.45 Notes to the financial statements should be used to add further explanation or analysis where required. It is preferable to summarize items in the R&P account and the Statements of Assets and Liabilities in order that they may show the overall position of the PCC more clearly and easily. If too much detail is included they become cluttered and difficult to read; such detail should be dealt with in the Notes.

7.46 As detailed in para 7.7 above, the accounting basis and policies must be detailed and it is usual to do this in the first Notes to the Financial Statements.

7.47 Notes are seldom necessary, although if notes would help the reader to understand the accounts better, they should be added. Examples of notes that may be included are:

- information about significant non-monetary resources, for example donated goods and services;
- a brief note on transactions with related parties and trustees;

- details of any remuneration or expenses paid to any trustee or related party; and
- details of the movement on particular restricted funds (where this may be useful to donors who stipulated how money was to be spent).

These matters may alternatively be included in the Trustees' Annual Report if separate notes to the accounts are not prepared.

Examples

7.48 Examples of various forms of financial statement are shown in Chapter 14.

chapter 8

Accounts on the accruals accounting basis

8.1 This chapter is addressed to PCCs who are preparing their financial statements on an accruals basis. It is appropriate both for PCCs which must prepare accruals accounts and for smaller PCCs which opt to prepare their financial statements on this basis even though their gross income is less than the accruals accounts threshold and to do so is not mandatory. This chapter is not for PCCs preparing accounts on the R&P basis, for whom guidance is provided in Chapter 7.

8.2 This chapter gives guidance on accounting for the types of transaction which most PCCs will encounter. It provides guidance on applying SORP 2005 in the context of the PCC but does not have the status of the SORP itself. A few PCCs, particularly the more complex (those with substantial investment assets or trading activities), should consult SORP 2005 to obtain authoritative guidance on specific points.

8.3 This chapter assumes that the reader is already familiar with the basic principles of the preparation of financial statements on the accruals basis.

SORP and the law

8.4 As explained in Chapter 1, PCCs are subject to the legal requirements of the Charities Act 1993, even though they are currently charities excepted from registration. Accordingly, they are required to comply with the Charity Accounting Regulations which bring into force the accounting and auditing requirements of Part VI of the Act. The Church Accounting Regulations 2006 create a compatible regime to the requirements of the Charities (Accounts and Reports) Regulations 2005 and should be complied with by all PCCs. Accounts on the R&P basis are explained in Chapter 7 and do not have to conform to the Regulations.

8.5 The Charities (Accounts and Reports) Regulations 2005 oblige PCCs who are preparing accruals accounts to disclose in the notes to the financial statements particulars of any material departure from the Regulations, accounting standards and SORP 2005. Also, those PCCs over the audit threshold must show their expenditure in the financial statements under specified activity headings.

8.6 The Church Accounting Regulations 2006 require compliance with SORP 2005 or its current equivalent.

General principles

Accounts structure

8.7 The financial statements are a report in financial terms on the activities and resources of the charity, and must comprise:

- **A Statement of Financial Activities** (SOFA) for the year that shows all resources made available to the PCC and all expenditure incurred by it, and reconciles all changes in its funds.

The Statement should consist of a single set of accounting statements and be presented in columnar form where the PCC has restricted or endowment funds, see table page 39.

- **A balance sheet** that shows the assets, liabilities and funds of the charity. SORP 2005 also comments that the balance sheet may be presented in columnar format. This is not mandatory but using it ensures the presentation of the required analysis of assets and liabilities by category of fund.

The balance sheet (or the notes to the financial statements) should also explain in general terms how the funds may or, because of restrictions imposed by donors, must be utilized.

- **Notes to the financial statements**, explaining the accounting policies adopted and explaining or expanding upon the information contained in the accounting statements referred to above or which provide further useful information. This will include notes analysing the figures in the financial statements and explaining the relationships between them.

8.8 The financial statements should include all the money and other assets entrusted to the PCC for whatever purpose and show how they have been expended during the year and how the unexpended balance of each fund is held at the end of the accounting period.

8.9 The corresponding figures for the previous year should be provided in the financial statements in accordance with generally accepted accounting practice, i.e. adjusted where necessary to show them on the same basis as the current year's figures.

The principle of materiality

8.10 'Materiality' is the principle which ensures that transactions or amounts that are clearly insignificant need not be separately shown or explained in the report or financial statements (see Glossary: 'material'). As a general rule, a transaction or amount may be treated as insignificant ('immaterial') if it is without doubt too trivial to influence the reader of the financial statements. Too much detail about small items may confuse the overall picture but, if there is doubt about whether or not something is 'material', the information should be included.

Accounting policies

8.11 In order to understand the figures in the financial statements, the reader needs to know the basis on which they have been prepared. The 'accounting policies' note to the financial statements should therefore disclose that the financial statements are prepared under the Church Accounting Regulations 2006 and in accordance with the Charities SORP (2005) and applicable accounting standards. In addition, the specific accounting policies and assumptions adopted for dealing with any material items should be briefly but clearly explained in the notes to the financial statements. They will include an explanation of the estimation techniques that have been used where judgement is required to record the value of incoming or outgoing resources and of assets and liabilities.

8.12 The accounting policies adopted must be appropriate to the PCC, and must also be consistent with the 'going concern' concept, namely that the PCC is a going concern and must include relevant, reliable, comparable and understandable information.

8.13 Observance of these fundamental concepts is presumed unless stated otherwise. In addition, the appropriateness of the individual accounting policies and estimation techniques adopted is to be judged by how well they enable the PCC's accruals accounts to achieve the following objectives, as set out in FRS 18 (Accounting Policies):

(a) relevance;

(b) reliability (which includes the concept of prudence in cases of uncertainty);

(c) comparability (which includes consistency); and

(d) understandability.

8.14 Apart from this, the accounting policies should indicate how the relevant accounting standards and recommendations have been applied in respect of any material items in the financial statements. They will help the reader to understand how matters noted in the paragraphs below have been handled in the financial statements and so they need to be included if they are to represent a true and fair view. A model set of accounting policies is set out at the end of this chapter. PCCs should add to and amend these as appropriate for their particular circumstances.

Summary Statement of Financial Activities

	Unrestricted Funds	Restricted Funds	Endowment Funds	Total Funds	Prior Year Total Funds
INCOMING RESOURCES					
Incoming resources from generated funds					
Voluntary income					
Activities for generating funds					
Investment income					
Incoming resources from charitable activities					
Other incoming resources					
TOTAL INCOMING RESOURCES					
RESOURCES EXPENDED					
Costs of generating funds					
Costs of generating voluntary income					
Fund-raising trading: cost of goods sold and other costs					
Investment management costs					
Charitable activities					
Governance costs					
Other resources expended					
TOTAL RESOURCES EXPENDED					
NET INCOMING/OUTGOING RESOURCES BEFORE TRANSFERS					
Transfers					
Gross transfers between funds					
Net incoming resources before other recognized gains and losses					
Other recognized gains/losses					
Gains on revaluation of fixed assets for charity's own use					
Gains/losses on investment assets					
Actuarial gains/losses on defined benefit pension schemes					
NET MOVEMENT IN FUNDS					
Reconciliation of Funds					
Total funds brought forward					
Total funds carried forward					

Fund accounting

The need to distinguish between funds

8.15 As explained in Chapter 3 the requirement to separate unrestricted, restricted and endowment funds applies to all PCCs regardless of size. The main purpose of the financial statements is to give a comprehensive view of all the resources made available to the PCC during the year and how they have been expended, with a balance sheet to show the overall financial position at the year-end. However, there are additional requirements for PCCs that have to account for restricted income and endowment funds. They need to account for the proper administration of the individual funds in accordance with their respective terms of trust.

Transfers between funds

8.16 In disclosing details of movements of funds, transfers affecting restricted funds should be shown separately from transfers to designated unrestricted funds. Material transfers out of and into restricted funds should be separately disclosed, without netting off, and should be accompanied by a narrative explanation of the nature of the transfer or allocation and the reason for it.

Particulars of individual funds

8.17 The summary of funds given in the SOFA and balance sheet should be supplemented by a statement in the notes showing the movement on material funds and an explanation of what the funds are to be used for. The reason for any funds being in deficit, and the actions proposed to correct this situation, should also be given in notes.

The Statement of Financial Activities (SOFA)

Format

8.18 The Statement should summarize for the year all incoming resources of the PCC, both capital endowment and income, and all resources expended by it, analysed in accordance with their nature or by activity (see below), and distinguishing between that relating to endowment funds, restricted income funds and unrestricted income funds, and should reconcile all movements in the funds since the previous 31 December.

8.19 The Statement should be supported by notes summarizing the movements in significant individual funds.

8.20 SORP 2005 requires that charities over the audit threshold should analyse their incoming resources and resources expended by Activity. The SORP also provides (appendix 5.3) that charities below the audit threshold may use any analysis of incoming and outgoing resources that may be best suited to their circumstances. Chapter 6 sets out how PCCs can group their incoming resources and resources expended into the SORP Activity categories and it is recommended that PCCs should, as far as possible, follow this approved layout as this has been designed to cover most of the PCC's activities and sources of funding. This layout will also provide the information needed to complete the annual return to the diocese.

8.21 Headings may be omitted where there is nothing to report in both the current and preceding periods.

8.22 Within the two separate sections of 'incoming resources', and 'resources expended', the individual sub-headings may be changed in order to present a true and fair view of the PCC's activities.

Incoming resources summary

8.23 All incoming resources becoming available to the PCC during the year must be summarized, distinguishing between those belonging to its unrestricted funds, its restricted income funds and its endowment funds. These should be classified in accordance with the activity headings set out in Chapter 6, namely:

Incoming resources

Incoming resources from generated funds

Voluntary income

Activities for generating funds

Investment income

Incoming resources from charitable activities

Other incoming resources.

These comprise the **total incoming resources**, but not necessarily the 'gross income' (see Chapter 2).

8.24 In the notes to the financial statements, endowment fund incoming resources should be analysed between permanent endowment and expendable endowment.

8.25 The summary should enable the reader of the financial statements to gain an accurate appreciation of the principal elements of the incoming resources of the charity, but should not be excessively detailed. Supporting analyses should be provided in notes to the financial statements.

Expenditure summary

8.26 All expenditure should be included in the SOFA as soon as it is incurred.

8.27 The expenditure summary should distinguish between various types of expenditure in a way that is appropriate to the PCC's activities, and between fund types (with supplementary analysis of any individual major funds by way of note). Subject to the same audit threshold relaxation for incoming resources detailed in 8.20 above, recommended activity classifications to be adopted are set out below as in Chapter 6, namely:

Resources expended

Costs of generating funds:

- Costs of generating voluntary income
- Fund-raising trading: cost of goods sold and other costs
- Investment management costs

Charitable activities

Governance costs

Other resources expended

These normally comprise the **total expenditure** (see Chapter 2).

Depreciation of fixed assets held for the PCC's own use

8.28 Fixed assets held for functional (church) use which are included in the balance sheet and are considered to have a finite useful life should be depreciated at annual rates to spread their cost to the PCC evenly over their useful life in each case. An example of such assets is a computer used in the church office. In addition, if recently acquired movable church furnishings are included (because they have either been valued or recently acquired), they should also be depreciated.

PCCs should consider whether it is necessary to capitalise and depreciate fixed assets of small value. Many PCCs set a threshold (of perhaps £500 or £1000) below which fixed assets are written off rather than capitalised.

8.29 This depreciation should be included in the appropriate cost category as annual expenditure provisions in the SOFA, and will appear in the balance sheet as accumulated depreciation deducted from the value of the relevant fixed assets.

8.30 To achieve the correct attribution of depreciation and to identify the nature of fixed assets held, fixed assets should be divided between those used in direct furtherance of the PCC's objects (for example, church halls and curates' houses) and those which are used for some other purpose, such as the generation of income (for example, a house available for rent). If a house is held purely to generate rent then it will be an investment property and generally will not be depreciated.

8.31 Where a fixed asset used for the functioning of the PCC and included at a value in the balance sheet has suffered permanent diminution in value or 'impairment' (this is unlikely to be a frequent occurrence), the loss should be recognized by means of an impairment charge in the SOFA.

8.32 In determining whether the balance sheet value of any individual asset has become 'impaired', changes in the value of other assets should not be taken into account.

Transfers between funds

8.33 Each column in the SOFA should be totalled to show the net incoming/outgoing resources before transfers. If the PCC has restricted income funds or endowment funds, or if designated funds are shown separately in the SOFA, any transfers between funds should be shown as a separate line. Transfers between the different classes of funds should not be netted off, but should be shown gross, with supporting explanations in the notes. Transfers should, of course, net off in the total column.

Net incoming resources for the year

8.34 Each column should again be totalled to give 'Net incoming resources before other recognized gains and losses'. The gains and losses should be recorded. Such gains and losses will form part of the fund in which the asset was held. The following should be recorded separately:

(a) revaluation gains on fixed assets held for use by the Church (for example, a curate's house);
(b) gains and losses on the revaluation and disposal of investment assets.

It is not necessary to split the investment gain between realized and unrealized categories.

Each column of the Statement will then be totalled to show the net movement in funds of the PCC for the year as shown in the example in Chapter 14.

Reconciliation of funds

8.35 To the net movement in funds for the year for each column should be added the total funds brought forward from the previous balance sheet, to show the amounts of the total funds carried forward as shown in the balance sheet at the year-end.

Comparative figures

8.36 In the Statement of Financial Activities, corresponding amounts for the previous year are required only for the total for each line, but it may help the reader if it is shown fund by fund wherever separate supporting movement statements are provided elsewhere (i.e. by way of note) for any of the underlying funds.

Accounting for incoming resources

Recognition in the Statement of Financial Activities

8.37 Members of the PCC have a legal duty to take proper care of everything that they are entrusted with, which means everything to which the PCC becomes entitled as soon as this entitlement becomes legally enforceable. This includes not only actual receipts of the year but also any money or other property – whatever its source or purpose – which could have been received if the PCC had exercised its legal right to take possession of it. It should be accounted for as incoming resources of the PCC for the year.

8.38 The value of all resources – both for income and endowment funds – accruing to the PCC should be recorded in the Statement of Financial Activities as soon as it is prudent and practicable to do so. In all cases incoming resources should not be recognized until the conditions for receipt have been met and there is reasonable assurance of receipt. This will be dependent on the following three factors being met:

(a) entitlement – normally arises when a particular resource is receivable or the PCC's right to it becomes legally enforceable;
(b) certainty – when there is reasonable certainty that the incoming resource will be received;
(c) measurement – when the monetary value of the incoming resource can be measured with sufficient reliability.

Donor-imposed restrictions

8.39 Where either incoming resources are given specifically to provide a fixed asset or a fixed asset is donated (a gift in kind), the PCC will normally have entitlement to the incoming resources when they are receivable. At this point, all of the incoming resources should be recognized in the Statement of Financial Activities and not deferred over the life of the asset. The possibility of having to repay the incoming resources does not affect their recognition in the first instance.

Once acquired, the use of the asset will be either restricted or unrestricted. If the use of the asset is restricted it will be held in a restricted fund. If its use is unrestricted the trustees may consider creating a designated fund reflecting the book value of the asset. The relevant fund (restricted or unrestricted) will then be reduced over the useful economic life of the asset in line with its depreciation.

8.40 When a PCC receives a gift, bequest or grant it will account for it, in either an unrestricted or restricted fund, once it is entitled to it and there are no conditions attached to its receipt. A condition which prevents entitlement must be one outside the PCC's control (such as obtaining matched funding or that the funds may only be expended in a later accounting period). When such a condition applies, the receipt should not be included in the SOFA until the condition has been met (i.e. until the money can lawfully be spent). The amount of such 'deferred income' will instead be shown in the balance sheet as a liability. The financial statements notes should explain all movements in 'deferred income', to enable the reader to understand the implications.

Legacies

8.41 Legacies receivable should be included in the SOFA in accordance with the general principles for the recognition of incoming resources. They should not be included until it is reasonably certain that they will be received and the amount can be measured with sufficient reliability.

8.42 Where the PCC is aware of an entitlement to a material legacy which has not been included in the financial statements, this fact and an estimate of the amount receivable should be disclosed in the notes to the financial statements.

Gifts in kind

8.43 Where material these should be included in the SOFA as follows:

(a) Assets given for use by the charity, e.g. photocopier for use in the church office, should be recognized as incoming resources when receivable.

(b) Where a gift has been made in kind but on trust for conversion into cash and subsequent application by the PCC, the incoming resource should normally be recognized in the accounting period when receivable; but in certain cases this will not be practicable. In these cases the income should be included in the accounting period in which the gift is sold.

8.44 In all cases the amount at which gifts in kind are brought into account should be either a reasonable estimate of their value to the PCC or the amount actually realized. The basis of any valuation should be disclosed. Where material, an adjustment should be made to the original valuation upon subsequent realization of the gift.

Donated services and facilities

8.45 A PCC may receive assistance in the form of donated facilities, beneficial loan arrangements, donated services (such as the provision of office accommodation where the rental is paid by a third party or the free use of telephone facilities) or services from volunteers. Such incoming resources should only be included in the SOFA where the benefit to the PCC is reasonably quantifiable and measurable. Donated services and facilities include those normally provided by an individual or entity as part of their trade or profession for a fee, but will exclude the value of contribution from volunteers as their contribution cannot be reasonably quantified in financial terms.

The cost in the SOFA should be the estimated value to the PCC of the service or facility received. This will be the price the PCC estimates it would pay in the open market for a service or facility of equivalent utility to the PCC. An equivalent amount should be included in the SOFA as expenditure under the appropriate heading. As a result both the value of this incoming resource and its contribution to the application of resources is recognized.

8.46 Most PCCs receive substantial amounts of voluntary help. Such help should not be accounted for in the SOFA, but should be referred to in the annual report.

Cost of generating funds

8.47 Voluntary income raised by the PCC should be brought into account gross, and associated costs should be accounted for as fund-raising expenditure.

Grants receivable

8.48 Receipts by way of grant should be treated in a similar manner to other incoming resources. They should be dealt with in the SOFA in accordance with the terms of the grant. This means, for example, that grants intended for specific purposes should be accounted for as restricted funds. Grants received as ordinary funds but designated by the PCC to specific purposes should be included as receipts in unrestricted funds, then as a transfer from unrestricted to designated funds.

8.49 Grants should not be recognized until the conditions for receipt have been complied with. Once these conditions are met the grant should be recognized even if the resources are received in advance of expenditure or there is a condition that all or part of the donation may be repaid to the donor. If repayment is possible then, depending on the probability, it should be noted as a contingent liability or recognized as an actual liability.

Trading activities

8.50 Some churches carry on trading activities such as letting church premises, selling books, producing magazines and running community cafés. Some of these activities may be outside the PCC's objects and care should be taken with major trading activities in case it is appropriate to form a separate trading company for liability and tax reasons. All proceeds of trading should be recognized as income in the period in which the 'sale' took place and any associated costs should be included in expenditure at the same time. This accounting principle of 'matching' the costs involved and the revenues arising from the trading activity applies to any form of trading. It also applies where the trading is carried out purely in order to raise funds, and regardless of whether the trading is regular or permanent, or only occasional. Where goods are purchased in one period but not sold until a later period, they should be shown in the balance sheet as stocks, in current assets, and charged to expenditure when the sale takes place.

8.51 Trading which is part of the PCC's charitable objects to further the work of the church (such as fee income, income from hall letting for church purposes and the sale of religious books) should be separated from fund-raising trading (such as selling postcards and souvenirs to tourists).

8.52 Some 'trading' involves merely the disposal of gifts in kind donated to the church (such as cakes for a cake stall or clothing for a rummage sale). In economic terms these are similar to trading and the proceeds must be treated as activities for generating funds.

8.53 Unless the cost of the trading activity is immaterial it is not acceptable simply to show the net trading result (profit or loss) in the SOFA.

8.54 If more than one trading activity is undertaken, then each significant activity should be separately disclosed, but this can be done in the notes.

8.55 All forms of trading should be recognized in this manner if significant, not merely activities that fall into the definition of trading for Income Tax or Value Added Tax purposes.

Disposal of fixed assets used for the functioning of the PCC

8.56 Any net gain arising on disposal of fixed assets (the sale proceeds less the book value) previously used by the PCC for its functional purposes (such as the curate's house or the office photocopier) should be included in the SOFA as an incoming resource of the fund concerned. If a net loss arises for the year, it should be included as an additional depreciation charge of the fund concerned under the appropriate heading of charitable or other expenditure. If material, the gains and losses should be disclosed separately, with a supporting note by way of explanation.

8.57 The accounting treatment of gains and losses arising on revaluation of fixed assets is a complex issue which is not covered in this chapter. Those wishing to opt for revaluation of fixed assets should refer to the SORP (2005) for the accounting treatment entailed.

Netting off

8.58 All incoming resources should, as far as practicable, be reported gross. This means, for example, that expenditure on putting on a fund-raising event such as a fete should not be netted off against the funds raised unless it will not materially understate the gross incoming resources and gross resources expended. On occasions it may not be practicable to report the resources gross. In such a case the reason for netting off should be given in the notes and an estimate of the gross funds raised and the deducted expenditure given in the SOFA.

Accounting for tax recoverable

8.59 By the end of the year the PCC is likely to have received income on which tax can be reclaimed. The tax repaid or repayable must be recognized in the financial statements, namely:

- any amounts that have been claimed and received from HMRC that relate to donations made during the period; and
- any amounts that have been claimed from HMRC but not yet received; and
- any amounts that could have been claimed at the year-end ('claimable').

8.60 Tax repayable to the PCC should be included in the SOFA in the same period as the income to which it relates, and disclosed separately as shown in Chapter 6. Any tax not received at the end of the year should be accounted for as a debtor until the PCC recovers the amount involved.

The balance sheet

Structure

8.61 The assets and liabilities should be analysed in the balance sheet between fixed assets (including investments and investment properties), current assets, current and long-term liabilities.

8.62 In particular, fixed assets should be subdivided between:

(i) tangible assets for the PCC's own use, which must be analysed in the notes between:
  (a) freehold interests in land and buildings;
  (b) leasehold and other interests in land and buildings;
  (c) plant and machinery, including motor vehicles;
  (d) fixtures, fittings and equipment;
  (e) payments on account and assets in course of construction.

(ii) heritage assets – see Chapter 5

(iii) investments, with supporting analysis of any significant holdings or properties in the notes.

8.63 All assets of material value held for use on a continuing basis in the PCC's activities should be classified as fixed assets for PCC use and included in (or excluded from) the balance sheet on the basis explained in Chapter 5. Most of these fixed assets are likely to be tangible assets, such as property or equipment, which are used in the course of the PCC's activities. Land and buildings held primarily for investment purposes should be classified as 'investment properties' and included with investments.

8.64 The notes to the financial statements should also summarize all changes in the amounts of each category of fixed assets as shown in the balance sheet and reconcile the opening and closing balances on each one.

This means separate reconciliations of the cost to date (or the valuation, where that option has been chosen) and of the depreciation or amortization provided. Similarly the notes should show the movements in investments (if any): carrying (market) value brought forward, plus additions at cost, less disposals at carrying value brought forward, plus or minus gain or loss on revaluation, equals carrying value carried forward.

8.65 Current assets should be subdivided by category, where applicable, to show:

(i) stock (for example heating oil, bookstall publications);

(ii) debtors, which should be further analysed in the notes between:

  (a) debtors for goods and services (for example rents receivable on premises letting);

  (b) amounts owed by an institution or body corporate which is a related party to the PCC;

  (c) other debtors (for example amounts owed by HMRC);

  (d) prepayments and accrued income.

(iii) investments (only applicable where the PCC intends to spend the proceeds of sale instead of reinvesting them); and

(iv) cash at bank and in hand (including deposits with the CBF Church of England Funds or a Diocesan Board of Finance).

The notes applicable to showing the movement in investments held as fixed assets also apply to investments held as current assets.

8.66 Liabilities should be analysed between those payable within a year (short-term) and others (long-term), with the total (if material) of any provisions for liabilities shown separately.

8.67 The totals for both short-term and long-terms creditors should be sub-analysed in the notes between:

(i) loans and overdrafts;

(ii) creditors for goods and services (for example, diocesan parish share – see below);

(iii) amounts owed to any institution or body corporate which is a related party to the PCC;

(iv) accruals and deferred income (for example, an estimate of fuel unbilled up to the year-end).

If a PCC has not met its obligations for parish share or quota payments in full for whatever reason but intends to do so in the future, outstanding payments should be included as a creditor in the balance sheet in accruals accounts.

If for whatever reason (usually by agreement) a PCC's obligations to pay parish share are not to be met in full, this fact should be mentioned in the annual report to enable a full understanding of the PCC's financial affairs.

8.68 The funds of a PCC should be grouped by kind, distinguishing between endowments, other restricted funds, designated and other unrestricted funds. The notes should distinguish any material individual funds among them.

8.69 In the notes to the balance sheet, the assets and liabilities representing those funds of the PCC should be clearly analysed between those funds. The notes should indicate whether or not sufficient resources are held in an appropriate form to enable each fund to be applied in accordance with the restrictions imposed. For example, if a PCC has a fund which is to be spent in the near future, it should be made clear in the notes whether or not the assets held in the fund are short-term assets.

8.70 In addition, the assets and liabilities should be analysed in a way that enables the reader to gain a proper appreciation of their spread and character. PCCs should not feel restricted by the formats provided in this chapter and are expected to provide more detail or analysis of the items concerned where this will lead to a better understanding of the financial statements. For example, long-term debtors (i.e. due only after more than one year) should, where the total is material, be separately stated in the balance sheet – otherwise their total amounts by category should be disclosed in the notes to the financial statements.

Balance sheet values

8.71 The assets and liabilities of a PCC should be included in the balance sheet at amounts determined on the following bases (see Chapter 5 for more information):

- fixed assets held for the PCC's functional use: cost (or valuation) less an appropriate provision for depreciation;
- fixed assets held for investment purposes (investments and investment properties): market value;
- current assets (other than investments): the lower of cost and net realizable value;
- liabilities: settlement value.

Capitalization of fixed assets

8.72 Details of certain fixed assets of the PCC (movable church furnishings) are recorded in the church Inventory irrespective of where they are physically located. As explained in Chapter 5 older items in the category of fixed assets may not need to be capitalized and recorded in the balance sheet but instead should be described in the notes to the financial statements.

8.73 Other than where it relates to consecrated buildings or benefice property, all new expenditure on the acquisition, enhancement, production or installation of fixed assets for use by the PCC and all other receipts of such fixed assets by way of gift that have a value above the threshold determined by the PCC, should be capitalized and included in the balance sheet. This general principle is not affected by the source of finance used to pay for the asset, or the source of finance likely to be used to pay for any future replacement of the asset.

8.74 The financial statements should be approved at a meeting of the PCC and the balance sheet signed and the date of approval shown. Only one signature is required, that of the chairman of the meeting. However, in the case of the Church of England, where the chairman of the meeting will normally be the minister, it is good practice for the financial statements also to be signed by one other member, normally the treasurer or churchwarden, to underline the joint responsibility of both the minister and the laity of the PCC.

Notes to the financial statements: other disclosures

Individual fund analysis

8.75 Movements in all the material underlying funds should be analysed in the notes to the financial statements, using the headings from, and reconciling with, the main SOFA. The constituent assets and liabilities of major individual funds should also be shown in the notes.

Charitable commitments

8.76 If an unfulfilled and non-contractual commitment to make a grant, payment or financial contribution to a third party either is a legally binding obligation, or a valid expectation was created in the mind of the third party at 31 December, it should be recognized in full as a liability in the financial statements for the year.

8.77 Where a PCC has authorized expenditure out of its unrestricted funds without making any binding commitment, the PCC may wish to designate unrestricted funds to represent this future expenditure commitment. Any such amounts should be shown separately as designated funds, and clearly explained in the notes to the financial statements. The notes should also explain why the PCC has set up such a fund.

8.78 Particulars of all material commitments should be disclosed in the notes if they have not been charged in the financial statements. The note should show the amounts involved, when the commitments are likely to be met and the movements on commitments previously reported.

8.79 Where later events make the recognition of liability no longer appropriate, the provision should be cancelled by credit against the relevant expenditure heading in the SOFA. The credit should mirror the treatment originally used to recognize the liability and should be disclosed separately, with a clear explanation in the notes to the financial statements, if material.

8.80 Disclosure or provision as appropriate may need to be made for any commitment the PCC may have in relation to the repair and maintenance of non-capitalized fixed assets such as benefice or consecrated property. If these amount to constructive obligations, they will be accounted for as creditors and charged to the SOFA. However, if there is no contractual commitment at the balance sheet date, any funds set aside for repair and maintenance should be regarded as designated funds and not charged to the SOFA. The annual report should in any case say when the last quinquennial inspection was held and give details of the immediate works needing completion.

Other commitments

8.81 Particulars of all other material binding commitments should also be disclosed. This may include, for example, operating leases for equipment or premises used by the church.

Loan liabilities secured on the PCC's assets

8.82 If any specific assets (whether land or other property) of the PCC are subject to a mortgage or charge given as security for a loan or other liability, a note to the financial statements should disclose (a) particulars of the assets which are subject to the mortgage or charge, and (b) the amount of the loan or liability and its proportion to the present value of the assets mortgaged or charged.

Contingent liabilities

8.83 A contingency existing at the year-end which as a result of some probable future event is considered likely to crystallize into a material liability should cease to be contingent and should be accrued in the financial statements. The amount of the liability should be capable of being estimated with reasonable accuracy at the date on which the financial statements are approved.

8.84 The notes should disclose the nature of each contingency, the uncertainties that are expected to affect the outcome, and a prudent estimate of the financial effect where an amount has not been accrued in the financial statements.

8.85 If such an estimate cannot be made, the financial statements should show why it is not practicable to make such an estimate.

Grants payable

8.86 If a PCC makes grants to institutions that are material in the context of its grantmaking, the PCC should disclose details of a sufficient number of these grants to provide an understanding of what the PCC has supported. The information given should include the name of the institution and total value of grants given.

8.87 The analysis should include the PCC's policy for making grants and show the nature of the institution receiving them. A breakdown similar to that shown in Chapter 6 would be satisfactory.

8.88 There is no requirement to disclose any grants if they are not material in relation to the PCC's total expenditure but PCCs will usually wish to disclose all their major contributions to other charitable bodies, whatever their value, and this is to be encouraged. These can be shown in the annual report or an attachment to it if not in the notes to the financial statements. Very exceptionally the disclosure of details of grants made to institutions could seriously prejudice the purposes of either the PCC or the recipient. The Charities SORP (para 209) explains what to do in these circumstances.

Transactions with members of the PCC and related parties

8.89 Where a PCC enters into any material transaction, contract or other arrangement (including a grant or donation) with any related party (see Glossary), the amounts involved and the terms and conditions should be disclosed in the notes to the financial statements. Certain transactions, including donations of any money or in kind from PCC members or those closely connected with them (as long as any terms of trust imposed cannot be seen as altering materially the way the PCC operates), benefice property maintenance and employee contracts, are unlikely to influence the separate independent interests of the charity and need not be disclosed. The total remuneration of employees is disclosed separately (see para. 8.94).

8.90 Any decision by the PCC to enter into a transaction should be, and should be seen to be, influenced only by the consideration of the Council's own interests. This is reinforced by charity law which, in certain circumstances, can invalidate transactions where the PCC has a conflict of interest. Therefore transactions with related parties (such as PCC members, their spouses and organizations connected with them) need to be disclosed. Transparency is particularly important where the relationship between the PCC and the other party or parties to a transaction suggests that the transaction could possibly have been influenced by interests other than the PCC's. It is possible that the reported financial position and results may have been affected by such transactions and, if that has happened, information about these transactions is therefore necessary for readers of the PCC's financial statements.

8.91 Contracts or similar arrangements directly or indirectly involving PCC members personally or persons with a close family or business connection with them should always be regarded as material and the amounts involved, together with the name of the PCC member, disclosed in the notes. Any personal benefit element must be separately disclosed. This includes details of the total salary costs where a PCC member is also a PCC employee. Where the members have received no such remuneration or other benefits, this fact should be stated.

8.92 Where travelling, subsistence or any other out-of-pocket expenses have been reimbursed to a member of the PCC or to a third party, the aggregate amount of all such expenses reimbursed should be disclosed in a note to the financial statements. The note should also indicate the nature of the expenses (e.g. travel, subsistence, entertainment, etc.) and how many of the members have been reimbursed for the year. Where the members have received no such reimbursement, this fact should be stated.

8.93 Sometimes PCC members act as agents for the PCC and make purchases on its behalf and are reimbursed for this expenditure, e.g. payment for stationery or candles. Such expenditure is not related to the services provided by a PCC member and there is no need to disclose it. Likewise there is no need to disclose routine expenditure that is attributable collectively to the services provided by the PCC, such as providing reasonable refreshment at a meeting.

Employee emoluments

8.94 The total staff costs showing the split between gross wages and salaries, employer's national insurance costs and pension costs and the average number of employees for the year, should be disclosed in the notes to the financial statements. Clergy paid through the diocese are not PCC employees.

8.95 If the PCC is over the audit threshold then the notes should also show the number of employees (if any) whose emoluments for the year fell within each band of £10,000 from £60,000 upwards.

Auditors' and independent examiners' remuneration

8.96 The notes to the financial statements should disclose separately the amount payable to the auditor or independent examiner in respect of:

(a) audit or independent examination services;

(b) other financial services such as taxation advice, consultancy, financial advice and accountancy, disclosing the fees separately under each head.

Ex gratia payments

8.97 The total amount or value of any

(a) payment or

(b) non-monetary benefit or

(c) other expenditure of any kind or

(d) waiver of rights to property

to which a PCC is entitled, which is made not as an application of funds or property for the general purposes of the PCC but in fulfilment of a compelling moral obligation, should be disclosed in the notes to the financial statements.

Support costs

8.98 Support costs are those incurred in undertaking an activity that, whilst necessary to deliver an activity, do not themselves produce or constitute the output of the charitable activity. Similarly, costs will be incurred in supporting income generating activities such as fund-raising, and in supporting the governance of the charity. They include generic costs such as payroll administration, accounting costs and computer maintenance. Since they do not constitute an activity but instead enable activities to be undertaken, they are allocated to the relevant activity cost category they support according to the following principles:

- Where appropriate, expenditure should be allocated directly to an activity cost category.
- Items of expenditure which contribute directly to more than one activity cost category should be apportioned on a reasonable, justifiable and consistent basis, e.g. the cost of a staff member whose time is divided between a fund-raising activity and a charitable activity should be apportioned on the basis of time spent on the particular activities.

There are a number of bases for apportionment that may be applied. Examples include:

- usage, e.g. electricity costs for the church, the hall and the presbytery;
- per capita;
- floor area;
- time.

There should be a note to the financial statements that provides details of the total support costs incurred. If there are material items or categories of expenditure within this total these should be separately identified. It is recommended that a grid is used that lists the activities and the separately identifiable material support costs that have been allocated.

If support costs are material, an explanation of how these costs have been allocated to each of the activity cost categories, i.e. the allocation basis, should be provided in the notes.

Cash flow statement

8.99 The largest PCCs may also have to provide a cash flow statement under FRS1. Such parishes will already require a full audit and the registered auditor will advise accordingly.

Model set of accounting policies

PCCs should adapt these as necessary. The accounting policies should be disclosed in the financial statements to assist the reader, particularly in respect of material items.

The financial statements have been prepared in accordance with the Church Accounting Regulations 2006 together with applicable accounting standards and the Charities SORP 2005.

The financial statements have been prepared under the historical cost convention except for the valuation of investment assets, which are shown at market value.

Funds

General funds represent the funds of the PCC that are not subject to any restrictions regarding their use and are available for application on the general purposes of the PCC. Funds designated for a particular purpose by the PCC are also unrestricted.

Restricted funds are those funds that must be spent on restricted purposes and details of the funds held and restrictions are provided in note xx. Endowment funds, where the capital must be retained, are explained in note xx.

The financial statements include all transactions, assets and liabilities for which the PCC is responsible in law. They do not include the financial statements of church groups that owe their main affiliation to another body, nor those that are informal gatherings of church members.

Incoming resources

Voluntary income and capital sources

Collections are recognized when received by or on behalf of the PCC.
Planned giving receivable under Gift Aid is recognized only when received.
Tax recoverable on Gift Aid donations is recognized when the donation is recognized.
Grants and legacies to the PCC are accounted for as soon as the PCC is notified of its legal entitlement, the amount due is quantifiable and its ultimate receipt by the PCC is reasonably certain.
Funds raised by the fête, garden party and similar events are accounted for gross.
Sales of books and magazines from the church bookstall are accounted for gross.

Other income

Rental income from the letting of church premises is recognized when the rental is due.

Income from investments

Dividends are accounted for when due and payable, and interest entitlements are accounted for as they accrue. Tax recoverable on such income is recognized in the same accounting year.

Gains and losses on investments

Realized gains or losses are recognized when investments are sold.
Unrealized gains or losses are accounted for on revaluation of investments at 31 December.

Resources used

Grants

Grants and donations are accounted for when paid over, or when awarded, if that award creates a binding obligation on the PCC.

Activities directly relating to the work of the Church

The diocesan parish share is accounted for when due. Any parish share unpaid at 31 December is provided for in these financial statements as an operational (though not a legal) liability and is shown as a creditor in the balance sheet.

Fixed assets

Consecrated property and movable church furnishings

Consecrated and beneficed property of any kind is excluded from the financial statements by s.96(2)(a) of the Charities Act 1993.

Movable church furnishings held by the vicar and churchwardens on special trust for the PCC and which require a faculty for disposal are accounted for as inalienable property unless consecrated. They are listed in the Church's inventory, which can be inspected (at any reasonable time). For inalienable property acquired prior to (2000) there is insufficient cost information available and therefore such assets are not valued in the financial statements. Items acquired since 1 January (2000) have been capitalized and depreciated in the financial statements over their currently anticipated useful economic life (initially over xx years) on a straight-line basis.

All expenditure incurred in the year on consecrated or beneficed buildings, individual items under (£1,000) or on the repair of movable church furnishings acquired before 1 January (2000) is written off.

(PCCs should fix the amounts or dates as appropriate to their circumstances.)

Other fixtures, fittings and office equipment

Equipment used within the church premises is depreciated on a straight-line basis over four years. Individual items of equipment with a purchase price of £1,000 (PCCs should fix a figure appropriate to their circumstances) or less are written off when the asset is acquired.

Investments

Investments are valued at market value at 31 December.

Current assets

Amounts owing to the PCC at 31 December in respect of fees, rents or other income are shown as debtors less provision for amounts that may prove uncollectable.

Short-term deposits include cash held on deposit either with the CBF Church of England Funds or at the bank.

chapter 9

The annual report

9.1 This chapter should be read by all PCCs.

The requirements

9.2 The preparation of a written annual report, like the preparation of the financial statements, is the joint responsibility of the whole PCC. It puts all the PCC's financial statements into perspective and relates them to the wider life of the church. It will review the past year and link financial plans to the vision for the future. For this reason, while it is legally a separate document from the financial statements, they should always be presented together in the same publication.

9.3 The Church Representation Rules (Rule 9(1)(b)) require 'an annual report on the proceedings of the parochial church council and the activities of the parish generally' to be received by the Annual Parochial Church Meeting (APCM). The meeting is then free to discuss it.

9.4 The report is quite separate from the statement or address that the incumbent may wish to make to the APCM.

9.5 The Church Accounting Regulations 2006 no longer contain specific requirements as to the information to be included in the annual report, but simply refer to the need to comply with the Charities Act, any regulations made thereunder and SORP 2005. The detailed requirements are set out in paragraphs 9.25 to 9.33.

9.6 The report will usually be drafted by the secretary and the treasurer of the PCC, but some PCCs may wish to involve others in the drafting. It is a significant document in the life of the church and should be prepared in that light rather than as a chore to be completed.

9.7 The PCC must adopt the report before it is presented to the APCM and it must be dated and signed by the chairman of the PCC meeting at which it was adopted. Ideally an early draft should be shown to the PCC, but beware attempting to draft by committee.

9.8 The independent examiner or the auditor will need to see at least a draft of the report as a part of their scrutiny of the financial statements.

9.9 The annual report should be attached to the financial statements whenever a full set of financial statements is distributed, together with a copy of the audit or independent examination report.

9.10 Because the report must be written for the general public as well as for church members, it has to include information that church members might take for granted, such as identification of the parish church, how the PCC operates and the names of its members.

9.11 The whole report should deal with the main activities of the church and new developments planned. It will give a flavour of the church at worship, 'being' as well as 'doing', in pastoral and mission modes, and how it relates to those outside and on the fringes as well as in the congregation.

9.12 It is in no one's interest to make the report long and complicated. It is much more likely to be read if it is succinct and to the point. PCCs that have access to computers and desk top publishing facilities will want to make the layout attractive and may wish to include graphs, graphics and photographs.

Risk management

9.13 Larger PCCs which are over the audit threshold are required to state in their annual report that the major risks to which the PCC is exposed have been reviewed and that systems or procedures designed to manage those risks have been established. This is the responsibility of the PCC.

9.14 Whilst PCCs with a gross income of less than £250,000 are not required to do this, it is best practice for all PCCs to be aware of the risks to which they are exposed and it is strongly recommended that all PCCs make a report.

9.15 The following is a brief introduction to the subject and larger PCCs may need to read more widely. A considerable amount of guidance has been published on the subject, including the Charity Commission guidance, which is available on their website. A number of individual dioceses have also published information to help PCCs.

We live our lives surrounded by risk.

- Toddlers risk injuring themselves by falling down stairs or being scalded by food being cooked in a kitchen. Their parents are likely to regard the impact of this, should it happen, as catastrophic. Moreover, the probability of the event is quite high. They therefore implement preventative controls (child gates to the kitchen and the stairs).
- Adults are at risk of injury from motor vehicles each time they cross the road. The impact of being knocked down could be severe. The probability is low. So some precautionary measures might be taken, such as using marked crossing points and the Green Cross Code. The consequences of being knocked down might be reduced by taking out insurance for accidental injury.

9.16 Individuals balance the effort required to take action with the probability and consequences of not taking action, often without thinking about it. Similarly, organizations respond to risk without considering the costs and possible implications. A sensible person will, from time to time, sit down and consider his/her responsibilities and what might happen to prevent them being fulfilled. Risk management is the equivalent process for an organization.

9.17 Risks to the achievement of the organizational objectives are identified and decisions taken on how best to manage them by taking measures to:

- try and prevent the event happening at all;
- reduce the probability that it will happen;
- reduce the impact on the achievement of the organization's objectives;
- stop undertaking the activity;
- share the risk, e.g. by insurance.

9.18 Risk can be defined as 'the threat that an event or action will adversely affect an organization's ability to achieve its objectives and execute its strategies'. The term 'risk' can include any circumstances that may, or do, have an adverse effect on an organization's activities and is wider than financial matters. Risks relate not only to the negative consequences of a threat, but also to the impact of not taking advantage of opportunities.

9.19 One approach to the categorization of risk is as follows:

- **Financial risk** is the most common category of risk and it is possible to measure many non-financial risks in terms of financial impact. Financial risks can be managed through budgets and internal financial procedures as well as through strategic business and development plans and management accounts.
- **Reputational risk** can have an impact on parishes if, for example, unwelcome publicity hinders the mission of the Church.
- **Statutory and legal requirements** such as health and safety, employment law, Charities Act, child protection and associated difficulties, which could lead to high compensation payments arising from equal opportunities or health and safety claims.
- **Operational risk** relates to threats to the Church's ability to deliver its objectives owing, for example, to damage to the church building.

9.20 The dimensions of likelihood (or probability) and impact (or consequences) measure risk as illustrated in the chart, which also indicates the sort of response that might be required. As can be seen, impact is a more serious consideration than likelihood.

	Low likelihood (not expected to happen, frequency less than once every five years).	**Medium likelihood** (could well happen, frequency at least once every five years).	**High likelihood** (is happening now or expected to happen within the next year).
High impact (key organizational objectives not delivered as planned).	Establish contingency plans. Insure.	Establish contingency plans and preventative controls. Insure.	Abandon activity.
Medium impact (key operational objectives not delivered as planned).	Accept risk, establish detective controls, respond if threat materializes.	Establish preventative controls.	Establish preventative controls.
Low impact (plans and resources need adjusting to deliver objectives).	Accept risk, respond if threat materializes.	Accept risk, respond if threat materializes.	Establish preventative controls.

9.21 Some examples might include:

high impact/medium likelihood – fire in the vestry;

high impact/low likelihood – no one coming forward to act as sidespeople;

medium impact/medium likelihood – something goes missing from the church safe;

low impact/high likelihood – transport strikes prevent the clergy from travelling.

9.22 All organizations face risks and, rather than deal with them as they occur, it is better for the PCC to plan for and protect against the risks it can identify. No process can be guaranteed to identify all the risks that may arise. The process can start by:

- reviewing key risks in each area of activity;
- reviewing current systems;
- assessing the adequacy of current systems;
- reviewing interaction between risks in all areas;
- improve systems if necessary.

A risk register can be established and reviewed, perhaps, annually.

New matters in the SORP 2005

9.23 The 2005 revision of the SORP made a number of significant changes to the annual report which are designed to link more closely the objects, aims, objectives for the year, and activities planned for the year, with the outcomes achieved. The report should explain the governance and management structure and enable the reader to understand how the numerical part of the financial statements relates to the organizational structure and activities of the PCC. See example in Chapter 14.

9.24 The full content of the report is recommended as best practice for all PCCs, but for all those PCCs which are below the audit threshold there are significant reductions in the disclosures. Where a disclosure is optional for smaller PCCs it is marked with an asterisk.

Reference and administrative information

9.25 This information should be given each year; even though much of it may be the same as for the previous year, it may be recorded separately from the main body of the report:

- the full name (town/village and church dedication) of the PCC;
- the location of the church (or address if it has one) and the PCC correspondence address. This could be the church office (if there is one), that of the incumbent or of an officer of the PCC that can be made public;
- the names of all the members of the PCC who have served since the commencement of the financial year until the approval of the financial statements. The names of those who have left the PCC and the names of those who have replaced them should be given. This is a list of all those who have been trustees of the charity. Those who have been officers of the PCC should be indicated;
- the names and addresses of bankers, legal and other advisers to the PCC, and of the independent examiner or auditor;*
- the name of the person or persons to whom day-to-day management is delegated, e.g. the incumbent.*

Structure, governance and management

9.26 This section should make clear to the reader the legal framework within which the PCC operates, and how decisions are made. It should include:

- An explanation of how the PCC is constituted. For most PCCs this will be as shown below. However a PCC which is a team ministry or part of a united benefice should briefly outline how it is established here.

  > "The Parochial Church Council is a corporate body established by the Church of England. The PCC operates under the Parochial Church Council Powers Measure. The PCC is excepted by order from registering with the Charity Commission."

- If the PCC has any related trusts or charities, an explanation of the relationship of the PCC to these trusts.
- A statement that the appointment of PCC members is governed by and set out in the Church Representation Rules.
- The policies and procedures adopted for the recruitment, induction and training of PCC members. As the PCC has ultimate responsibility for a wide range of matters affecting the parish, including such matters as compliance with health and safety, disability discrimination legislation and child protection, it is important that the PCC adopts appropriate training procedures. These are likely to include training courses arranged by the diocese or deanery which are attended by a

PCC representative who reports back to the PCC as a body, and the dissemination of reading matter.*

- A brief description of the way the PCC organizes itself in order to carry out its aims and objectives. Many PCCs will probably have only a Standing Committee, but others may well have various committees. The purpose or terms of reference of the committees should be summarized. This should make clear the types of decision which are delegated to committees or to the incumbent or administrator.*
- A statement confirming that the major risks to which the PCC is exposed, as identified by the PCC members, have been reviewed and systems or procedures have been established to manage those risks.*

Objectives and activities

9.27 This section establishes the framework under which the PCC has operated in the year and its intentions. It should provide:

- a statement of the aims and objects of the PCC. The primary object of all PCCs will be the promotion of the Gospel of our Lord Jesus Christ according to the doctrines and practices of the Church of England. The PCC (Powers) Measure 1956 states the PCC 'is to co-operate with the minister in promoting in the parish the whole mission of the Church, pastoral, evangelistic, social and ecumenical'. Some parishes may have 'mission' or 'vision' statements they wish to add to this;
- an explanation of the PCC's main objectives for the year. These may, largely, remain constant from year to year, but may also include a particular focus for a year which may either have been determined by the PCC, such as particular work on the buildings; or be led by the deanery or diocese, such as mission and growth initiatives. The objectives set for the year need not relate to matters which can be 'closed' within the year but may form part of a longer term project;*
- an explanation of the strategies and activities that have been adopted to enable the PCC to achieve its objectives. This could provide details of the programmes the church does, such as regular worship services; house groups; women's, men's and youth groups; drop-in centres; outreach work; etc. The costs of these activities can be shown in the accounts and thus provide a direct link to the report;*
- an explanation of the contribution of volunteers where they play a significant role either in the charitable activities of the PCC or in generating funds. This might include an explanation of the activities undertaken and the contribution in terms of hours or staff equivalents and may also include an indicative value of this contribution. Similarly, where the PCC has received unquantifiable free facilities or services during the year, it should explain briefly the extent to which it relies on these continuing in order to pursue its work;*
- the policy for making grants or donations should be given (including how potential recipients are identified). It will be rare for a PCC to have social or programme related investment activities but where these exist the policies adopted for the selection and management of these activities should be given.*

Achievements and performance

9.28 For PCCs under the audit threshold, this section should provide a summary of the main achievements of the church in the year. This could include:

- Extracts from returns to the Diocese on numbers of different types of services held, attenders at the regular services, baptisms, confirmations, etc.
- Details of the various special activities that the church ran during the year, e.g. missions, fund-raising for overseas mission, pilgrimages, community events, etc.

For PCCs over the audit threshold this section sets out the outcomes from the planned strategies and activities in the year in the context of the objectives which the PCC set. This may include:

- a review of the charitable activities undertaken that explains the performance achieved against the objectives set. In some cases it will be possible to explain the outcomes in terms of numbers (such as numbers on the electoral roll and/or attendance figures). Much of the work of the church, however, cannot be reduced to numbers and in order to evaluate its achievements the PCC will need to draw on reports of experiences which may be oral or written. Where the objectives set cover a longer term than the financial year, the review will take the form of a progress report;
- where they are material, a review of the performance of fund-raising activities against the objectives set for them;*
- where material investments are held, details of investment performance against the investment objectives set;*
- a commentary on those factors within and outside the PCC's control that are relevant to the achievement of the objectives. These might include relationships with employees, members of the congregation, and the church's position in the wider community. This is intended to give a context to the activities of the year: for example the departure of the incumbent or a key member of staff may, necessarily, curtail some of the work planned for the year.*

Financial review

9.29 The report will paint a picture of the financial position of the church which will supplement the financial statements and assist the reader in understanding what it is that they are being asked to support financially and how those resources (and others) are being stewarded and used. (It should also review the financial position of any subsidiary undertakings the church may have.) This section of the report should also include:

- a statement of the PCC's policies on the reserves that are held (see 9.32–9.33) stating the level of reserves held and why they are held;
- an explanation of the circumstances that have given rise to any fund which is materially in deficit and details of any steps being taken to eliminate that deficit;
- details of the principal funding sources and how expenditure in the year under review has supported the key objectives of the PCC;*
- where material investments are held, the investment policy and objectives, including the extent to which social, environmental or ethical considerations are taken into account.*

Plans for future periods

9.30 For larger PCCs over the audit threshold the report should provide the reader with an explanation of the PCC's plans for the future (this will be the current year at the time the report is presented), including the key objectives and activities planned to support them. These will then form the basis of the objectives and activities section of the next report.*

Funds held as custodian trustees on behalf of others

9.31 In some circumstances the PCC may act as a custodian trustee (see Glossary) for the assets of another charity. Where this is the case the report should give a brief description of the assets held; the name and objects of the charity on whose behalf they are held and an explanation of how this fits with the objects of the PCC; and details of the arrangements for the safe custody and segregation of such assets from those of the PCC.

Reserves policy

9.32 The PCC should formulate and disclose its policy on reserves. Reserves are defined as that part of the PCC's income funds that is freely available. This definition of reserves therefore normally excludes:

(a) permanent endowment funds

(b) expendable endowment funds

(c) restricted income funds

and any part of unrestricted funds which is not currently available for spending, for example:

(d) income funds which can only be realised by disposing of fixed assets held for charity use.

Individual parishes may have more or less reserves than this simple calculation suggests. For example they may have expendable endowments that can be spent (increasing reserves) or they may have designated some part of general funds for a particular project (reducing reserves). PCCs should report the amount of their reserves in the report.

The adoption of a policy on reserves will help to identify situations where a PCC may need to consider either reducing or increasing the level of reserves that it holds. For example, the church may be in receipt of income that more than covers all its running costs (including diocesan parish share). Money collected from parishioners is therefore over and above what the parish needs. Alternatively, there may be parishes where the reserves are too low to cope with the requirements of the PCC's cash flow.

9.33 In addition to stating the amount of reserves held, the report should explain what the PCC considers to be an appropriate level of free reserves, and what action the PCC proposes to take to reduce or increase its free reserves where necessary. This will show the parish that it is acting responsibly in holding the level of reserves that it holds. The public can then fully understand the availability and planned use of the PCC's funds. Even if the PCC has no free reserves, it should provide an explanation of this.

chapter 10

The selection of an independent examiner

10.1 All PCCs below the audit threshold may choose to have their financial statements independently examined rather than audited. A major donor or grant maker may require the financial statements to be audited even though an independent examination might otherwise have been chosen. An audit is a more onerous form of scrutiny and must be carried out by a registered auditor but an auditor can be asked to act as an examiner. PCCs who can choose to prepare their financial statements on the R&P basis should normally choose independent examination rather than audit.

What does the PCC have to do?

10.2 A suitable examiner has to be appointed by the Annual Parochial Church Meeting (APCM). The PCC will have to consider carefully the suitability of a prospective independent examiner in good time to guide the meeting in its appointment.

Can an examiner be paid?

10.3 The PCC is entitled to pay a reasonable fee to an independent examiner for their services. If the services of a competent examiner cannot be obtained on a voluntary basis, the PCC should be prepared to pay a modest fee, which is a proper charge on its funds. The PCC should not be pressured into appointing a voluntary person just because they will do the work free of charge. It must be satisfied that they have the requisite ability and experience.

Who could be an independent examiner?

10.4 An independent examiner is described in section 43(3)(a) of the Charities Act 1993 as 'an *independent person* who is reasonably believed by the trustees to have the *requisite ability* and practical experience to carry out a *competent examination* of the financial statements'.

10.5 The term 'independent examiner' does not exclude an accountant or, indeed, a registered auditor, but recognizes that the scrutiny is less onerous than a full audit.

What does 'independent' mean?

10.6 For an examiner to be independent that individual must have no connection with the PCC which might appear to be prejudicial to an impartial examination of the financial statements.

10.7 The following persons will normally be considered to have a connection with the PCC that makes it inappropriate for them to be an examiner:

(a) a member of the PCC or any of its sub-committees (this exclusion is already included in the Church Representation Rules);

(b) an employee of the PCC, or a person receiving benefit or support from PCC funds by way of a gift (other than a fee received as an examiner);

(c) a close relative, business partner or employee of any person who falls within sub-paragraph (a) or (b) above.

10.8 An independent examiner can, however, be a member of the Church with their name on the electoral roll.

What is 'requisite ability'?

10.9 Whether an examiner has the requisite ability will depend very much on the size and complexity of the PCC's financial statements as well as on their individual experience. It will probably be appropriate for a person who has 'audited' the financial statements in the years before these new regulations came into force to continue to do so, provided they can satisfy the independence test. They will need to ensure that they understand their responsibilities under the legislation.

What sort of people can be appointed?

10.10 For smaller PCCs with a gross income and total expenditure of less than £10,000 and financial statements prepared on the R&P basis it may be appropriate, for example, to use anyone with basic bookkeeping skills to examine the financial statements. While the Church Accounting Regulations 2006 require an examination, the method of examination below £10,000 is not specified by the Charities Act.

10.11 For PCCs with a gross income up to £100,000 and with financial statements prepared on the R&P basis, an appropriate independent examiner would be someone more familiar with business and financial matters, but they need not be a qualified accountant.

10.12 It is recommended that PCCs with gross income between £100,000 and £250,000, or total assets in excess of £1,000,000 or who choose to prepare accruals accounts with a Statement of Financial Activities (SOFA), consider selecting a qualified accountant to carry out the independent examination.

10.13 When financial statements are prepared on the accruals basis an understanding of accountancy principles and accounting standards and practices will be needed in order to show the required true and fair view. The skills and experience of a qualified accountant will be desirable when substantial assets are held by a PCC.

10.14 Those who are suitably qualified to examine the financial statements of larger and more complex PCCs will also be suitable to examine the financial statements of smaller PCCs. While a qualified accountant is recommended for larger PCCs, examples of those who may be appropriate as one moves down the scale to the smaller PCCs are finance managers employed by large commercial organizations, through bank or building society managers or local authority treasurers to businessmen or schoolteachers.

How should an examiner's ability be checked?

10.15 The need to seek evidence of the ability of a prospective independent examiner will depend upon the size and complexity of the PCC's financial statements. There would normally be people in the community, such as those instanced above, who would be expected to have the necessary competence. If the prospective independent examiner is not known to the members of the PCC or if the turnover is greater than £100,000, PCCs should consider asking to see a CV, taking independent references and possibly forming a small group to interview candidates.

10.16 Difficulties can occur where the examiner has been recommended by an individual member of the PCC, who has then made the only contact with them. There have been cases where it was found that the examiner never existed!

What is appropriate 'practical experience'?

10.17 The PCC should satisfy itself that a prospective examiner has practical experience of preparing or reviewing and evaluating the financial statements of comparable organizations and can readily understand the PCC's financial statements. An examiner may have acted successfully as an independent examiner or auditor on previous occasions for other Churches or be responsible for financial decisions requiring mature judgement and relevant knowledge.

How can someone understand what is required in an examination?

10.18 The treasurer should discuss fully with the prospective examiner the work of the PCC and its expectations. Help will be found in these guidance notes on the duties of an examiner. In some dioceses guidance and advice may be available centrally, or treasurers in neighbouring parishes or deanery finance officers may be in a position to assist. The duties must be followed to ensure that the requirements of the Church Accounting Regulations 2006 are met. The Charity Commission has produced guidance on independent examinations in its publication CC63. This is available on its website.

What happens when the PCC and the APCM appoint an examiner?

10.19 Particularly for larger PCCs, it would be wise for the independent examiner to reduce the chance of any misunderstanding by writing to the PCC detailing its accounting responsibilities and the examiner's statutory responsibilities. The content of the letter should be agreed with the PCC and a sample letter is included with the examples in Chapter 14. It may be altered and sent from the PCC to the examiner.

10.20 Only examiners of PCCs with high income levels will probably document the agreed terms of engagement in this way, but the matters set out here should be discussed and agreed with all independent examiners prior to the examination.

10.21 It can be seen that the examiner should be given sufficient time in which to complete the examination.

10.22 The PCC will need to approve a motion for the appointment of the independent examiner at the APCM. A suitable form of words is:

> The PCC have elected to subject the financial statements to independent examination and therefore, having made appropriate enquiries, propose [*insert the name of the examiner*] as independent examiner until the next APCM.

chapter 11

The duties of an independent examiner

11.1 As explained in Chapter 1 the majority of PCCs will be required to have their financial statements subject to external scrutiny by an independent examiner. That chapter explains when this type of scrutiny can be carried out on the PCC's financial statements. Chapter 10 deals with the issues surrounding the appointment of an independent examiner.

11.2 This chapter explains the duties of independent examiners in carrying out their work and will enable PCCs to understand the scope of an independent examination.

11.3 The boxed paragraphs in bold type are Directions set out by the Charity Commission for carrying out independent examinations. In undertaking an independent examination an individual must follow these procedures and should be satisfied that each objective has been achieved by their work. Many dioceses are likely to help by giving training. A work programme for use for the examination of the financial statements of less complex PCCs is included at the end of this chapter. It may be photocopied for use.

11.4 Below each Direction, guidance and recommended procedures are provided. Although these procedures are not intended to be an exhaustive list and the individual circumstances of each examination performed must be considered, they are intended to be an indication of the level of work considered necessary in order for an independent examiner to be able to report on the financial statements examined.

Comparison of independent examination with audit

11.5 To many people an independent examination will be an unfamiliar term and they will not be aware of the differences between these two forms of external scrutiny of the PCC's financial statements.

11.6 Whilst both represent a formal examination of the financial statements by an independent individual, the level of scrutiny involved in an independent examination is considerably less than is involved with an audit. It is important to recognize that the procedures that may have been performed on PCC accounts in the past which have been termed 'audits' are in many situations likely to have been less formal than a professional audit, or even indeed than the new form of independent examination.

11.7 An independent examination involves a review of the accounting records kept by the PCC and a comparison of the financial statements presented with those records. It is a formal exercise which must be properly planned, controlled and recorded. It also involves a review of the financial statements and consideration of any unusual items or disclosures identified. Verification and vouching procedures only become necessary where material concerns or doubts arise from procedures, and where satisfactory explanations cannot be obtained from the PCC or its officers.

Examination and accounting thresholds

11.8 Carry out such specific procedures as are considered necessary to provide a reasonable basis on which to conclude that the PCC falls within the threshold for independent examination, as detailed in Chapter 1, and that a full audit by a registered auditor is not required.

11.9 The PCC may elect for independent examination rather than full audit, and may also elect for the preparation of R&P accounts rather than preparation of accruals accounts. For either election to be valid, the PCC must be within the relevant income and expenditure bands specified in the regulations for that election. The examiner should therefore ascertain:

- the PCC's gross income and total expenditure (see Chapter 2 for definitions) for the financial year concerned, as well as the two previous years;

- whether the governing document of organizations associated with the PCC stipulates any form of professional audit;
- whether any grant condition demands an audit; and
- whether all subsidiary funds have been included in the calculations.

11.10 Carrying out these procedures at an early stage, particularly if the PCC is likely to pass the £250,000 threshold, should prevent the work of the examiner being duplicated by a subsequent professional audit which would add to the expenses for the PCC.

11.11 In cases where the PCC's gross recorded income or total expenditure for the year of the financial statements, or either of the two years preceding, exceeds the threshold level of £250,000 the financial statements should be referred back to the PCC for an auditor to be appointed under the Church Accounting Regulations 2006, which state that the financial statements should be audited by a registered auditor or a person authorized by the Secretary of State to audit charity accounts.

11.12 Examiners should familiarize themselves with the threshold bands and their effect on the accounting procedures for PCCs. Where the financial statements comprise a R&P account and a Statement of Assets and Liabilities, prepared under the Church Accounting Regulations 2006, the examiner should begin by ascertaining that the gross income of the PCC does not exceed the £100,000 threshold for that year. If it appears that the threshold has been exceeded, the financial statements should be referred back to the PCC for preparation on an accruals accounting basis.

11.13 The examiner should consider at an early stage of the examination the levels of income and expenditure disclosed by the accounting records and by any trial balance. The examiner does, however, need to remain alert to any additional information which may come to his attention during the course of the examination that indicates that an income or expenditure threshold has been crossed. In particular, the examiner needs to identify any potential understatement or netting/offsetting of income and expenditure.

11.14 The level of income or expenditure should be calculated in accordance with the methods set out in Chapter 2. If financial statements are prepared on an accruals basis then the level of income or expenditure should be considered on an accruals basis. Where financial statements are prepared on the R&P basis then the level of income or expenditure should be considered on the basis of money actually received and expended.

Understanding the PCC

11.15 Obtain an understanding of the PCC's organization, accounting systems, activities and nature of its assets, liabilities, incoming resources and application of resources in order to plan the specific examination procedures appropriate to the circumstances of the PCC.

11.16 For a proper examination to be carried out it is important for the examiner to have an understanding of the operations, structure and objectives of the PCC, as laid down in accordance with the PCCs (Powers) Measure 1956 and Church Representation Rules. This understanding will help the examiner to plan appropriate examination procedures. The steps taken by an examiner would normally include:

- consideration of the PCC's objects, powers and obligations, which are set out in the PCCs (Powers) Measure 1956;
- discussions with the PCC or its representatives to ascertain the structure, methods and means by which the PCC seeks to achieve its objects;
- discussions with the PCC or its representatives about the affairs and activities of the PCC in order to gain an insight into any special circumstances and problems affecting the PCC;
- reviewing the minutes of PCC and relevant committee meetings to ascertain details of major events, plans, decisions and any changes in the PCC's officers; and

- obtaining details of accounting records maintained, methods of recording financial transactions and financial control arrangements.

Documentation

11.17 Record the examination procedures carried out and any matters which are important to support conclusions reached or statements provided in the examiner's report.

11.18 The independent examiner's working papers should provide details of the work undertaken and support any conclusions reached, and record any judgemental matters which may arise. Working papers should normally be retained by the examiner for six years from the end of the financial year to which they relate, and would normally include:

- a letter of engagement from the independent examiner to the PCC (an example letter is provided in Chapter 14);
- relevant information extracted or obtained from any governing document, PCC and other committee meeting minutes and a record of discussions with the PCC or its representatives;
- details of procedures carried out during the examination, with conclusions reached and any areas of concern identified;
- notes as to how any areas of concern have been resolved together with details of any verification procedures used;
- schedules showing the breakdown of accounting items that have been aggregated for accounts disclosure purposes;
- copies of any trial balance, financial statements and the PCC's annual report.

Comparison with accounting records

11.19 Compare the financial statements of the PCC with the PCC's accounting records in sufficient detail to provide a reasonable basis on which to decide whether the financial statements are in accordance with such accounting records.

11.20 It is necessary to compare the financial statements with the underlying accounting records. Where prepared on an accruals basis, all balances in the financial statements will need to be compared with the trial balance, analysed cash book or any nominal ledger maintained. Where financial statements are prepared on a R&P basis a direct comparison with the cash records of the PCC should be carried out if no nominal ledger is kept.

11.21 Test checks will also be necessary of the posting of entries from books of prime entry (e.g. cash book, petty cash book, services or offerings register, etc.) to any nominal ledger and/or to the trial balance itself. Similar checks are also necessary even where accounting records are maintained by using computer accounting packages as the internal integrity of such packages cannot be assumed.

11.22 A review of bank reconciliations, and any control accounts prepared, will provide a useful check as to the completeness and accuracy of posting from books of prime entry.

11.23 There is no requirement for accounting entries to be checked against source documents unless concerns arise during the course of the examination which cannot be resolved by seeking explanations.

11.24 Whilst the PCC is responsible for the preparation of financial statements, in some parishes the examiner may also prepare financial statements on behalf of the PCC. The preparation of financial statements will not generally impinge on his independence provided he ensures that the requirements of the Charity Commission's Directions are met and avoids involvement in the management or administration of the

PCC. Much of the work, such as posting checks, may have been carried out by the examiner in the course of the financial statements' preparation and the examiner should consider whether separate procedures as set out above are also necessary to ensure that this Direction has been met.

Accounting records

11.25 Review the accounting records maintained in accordance with section 41 of the Charities Act 1993 in order to provide a reasonable basis for the identification of any material failure to maintain such records.

11.26 The PCC is responsible for maintaining proper accounting records.

11.27 The examiner is required to review the accounting records with a view to identifying any material failure to maintain such records in accordance with section 41(1) of the Charities Act, which requires that they are sufficient to show and explain all the PCC's transactions, are capable of disclosing at any time the financial position of the charity with reasonable accuracy, and enable the PCC to ensure that any financial statements prepared by it comply with the form and content requirements set out in the Regulations.

11.28 The review procedures are not aimed at identifying the occasional omission or insignificant error but at any gross failure to maintain records in a manner consistent with statutory requirements.

11.29 Accounting records should be well organized and capable of ready retrieval and analysis. The records may take a number of acceptable forms: for example, book form, loose-leaf binder or computer records.

11.30 The accounting records should be up to date, should be readily available, and should provide the basic information from which the financial position can be ascertained, not only at the year-end, but on any selected date.

11.31 The accounting records should contain:

- details of all money received and expended, the date, and the nature of the receipt or expenditure; and
- details of assets and liabilities.

Smaller PCCs may not maintain formal ledgers to record assets and liabilities, and in such instances the requirements can generally be met by maintaining files for unpaid invoices and amounts receivable. A record of fixed assets is generally necessary to meet the accounting requirements. Some churches will maintain this record in the form of an 'inventory'. For more explanation of the fixed assets that may be held by a PCC, see Chapter 5.

Analytical procedures

11.32 Carry out analytical procedures to identify unusual items or disclosures in the financial statements. Where concerns arise from these procedures, the examiner must seek explanations from the PCC. If, after following such procedures, the examiner has reason to believe that in any respect the financial statements may be materially mis-stated then additional procedures, including verification of the asset, liability, incoming resource or application of resources, must be carried out.

11.33 It is important that the examiner looks carefully at the final financial statements to see if they reveal any unusual items, unexpected fluctuations, or inconsistencies with other financial information. This procedure is called analytical review. Steps taken would normally include:

- comparing the financial statements with those for comparable prior periods;
- comparing the financial statements with any budgets or forecasts that have been produced;
- considering whether incoming resources and the application of resources are consistent with known fund-raising sources, activities, and the objectives of the PCC. It is important to have obtained a

proper understanding of the nature of the PCC's activities and affairs for this aspect of the review to be successful;

- considering whether the liabilities and current assets disclosed are consistent with the scale and type of activity undertaken;
- considering whether fixed-asset investments are producing an income consistent with their size and nature; and
- considering whether the tangible fixed assets are consistent with the scale and type of activity undertaken by the PCC.

11.34 Where analytical review procedures identify any unusual item, unexpected fluctuation or inconsistency, then explanations should be sought from the PCC.

11.35 If the explanations provided by the PCC do not satisfy the examiner, then additional procedures will be necessary. Such procedures may include:

- comparison of amounts of planned giving with Gift Aid declarations held or Envelope Scheme records;
- direct confirmation from grant makers of amounts remitted to the PCC;
- physical inspection of a tangible fixed asset;
- verification of title to an asset (e.g. an investment certificate or title deeds);
- inspection of third-party documentary evidence (e.g. invoice, contract or agreement) to verify any expense or liability or to confirm an amount of income received or receivable;
- third-party certification of a bank balance, or other asset held, including the custody of investment certificates; and
- checking of a post-year-end receipt or payment to confirm recoverability of a debt or the amount of a liability.

11.36 A comprehensive list of analytical procedures, and of additional procedures where concerns arise is beyond the scope of this publication, and will to an extent be an area in which the examiner will need to exercise judgement and draw on experience.

Form and content of financial statements

11.37 Carry out such detailed procedures as the examiner considers necessary to provide a reasonable basis on which to decide whether or not the financial statements comply with the requirements of the Church Accounting Regulations 2006 as to the form and content of PCC financial statements.

Accruals basis

11.38 Where financial statements are prepared on an accruals basis, the Regulations lay down the requirements as to the form and content of such financial statements.

11.39 The examiner should be conversant with the Regulations as to the form and content of PCC financial statements and should examine the financial statements in sufficient detail to ensure compliance with these Regulations (but without regard to their requirement for a 'true and fair view' to be shown by the financial statements).

11.40 The Regulations draw heavily on the recommendations of the Statement of Recommended Practice – Accounting and Reporting by Charities (the Charities SORP).

11.41 Where the gross income of the PCC exceeds £100,000 and the financial statements are, therefore, drawn up on an accruals basis, a more detailed knowledge of the Charities SORP will be required as the notes to the financial statements of such charities will require a statement as to whether or not the financial statements have been prepared in accordance with any applicable accounting standards and statements of recommended practice. Further details for financial statements prepared on an accruals basis are provided in Chapter 8.

Receipts & Payments basis

11.42 The Regulations do not specify the form and content of financial statements prepared on a R&P basis. Guidance on the form and content of such financial statements can be found in Chapter 7. Whilst this chapter sets out best practice for the format of such financial statements, there is, however, no requirement for the examiner to carry out specific procedures to ensure compliance with that guidance.

Accounting policies, estimates and judgements

11.43 **When financial statements are prepared on an accruals basis, review the accounting policies adopted and consider their conformity with fundamental accounting concepts, consistency of application and their appropriateness to the activities of the PCC. The examiner must also consider and review any significant estimate or judgement that has been made in preparing the financial statements.**

Accruals basis

11.44 The accounting policies adopted, and also any estimates or judgements made in preparing the financial statements, may have a material effect on both the financial activities and state of affairs disclosed by the financial statements. Such matters, therefore, require careful consideration by the examiner.

11.45 The examiner should be satisfied that financial statements are prepared on a basis consistent with the going concern assumption and the accruals concept and that the accounting policies adopted conform to these concepts and are appropriate to the activities of the PCC and to ensure a relevant, comparable and understandable financial statements presentation. Model accounting policies are provided in Chapter 8.

11.46 The examiner must consider the reasonableness of any estimates or judgements where they are material to the financial statements. Matters that may require consideration include:

- the allocation of monies received to restricted or unrestricted funds;
- the inclusion of figures relating to subsidiary organizations such as fellowship groups and 'Friends' associations;
- transfers to or from designated fund accounts;
- valuation of gifts in kind;
- valuation of fixed-asset investments where no market prices exist;
- estimates resulting from transactions not being fully recorded in the accounting records; and
- where applicable, the allocation of costs between the various expenditure categories of the SOFA (see Chapter 6).

11.47 The values at which assets and liabilities are recorded in the financial statements are determined by the principles set out in the SORP 2005. Where the income of the PCC is less than £100,000, then guidance as to the application of the SORP can be obtained from Chapter 7. Where, however, income exceeds £100,000 or the PCC has complex investments, then reference should also be made to SORP 2005.

Receipts & Payments basis

11.48 The only fundamental accounting concept which applies is that of consistency. Accounting policies and judgemental issues have less relevance since the R&P account is simply a factual record of money actually received and expended. The Statement of Assets and Liabilities is a straightforward schedule of information. This direction therefore does not apply to such accounts, unless other examination procedures have given rise to concerns that need to be addressed in this way.

11.49 Further guidance as to the form and content of R&P accounts can be obtained from Chapter 7.

Events subsequent to the year-end

11.50 When accruals accounts are prepared, enquire of the PCC as to material events subsequent to the year-end of the financial statements examined that may require adjustment or disclosure in the financial statements.

Accruals basis

11.51 An event occurring after the balance sheet date may have a material effect on both the financial activities and state of affairs disclosed by the financial statements.

11.52 The events that have occurred subsequent to the year-end should therefore be discussed with the PCC. Any effects on the financial statements under review should be considered. The matters that should be discussed include:

- whether any income anticipated and accrued in the financial statements at the year-end has proved irrecoverable;
- discovery of an error or fraud;
- crystallization of any liability;
- repayment of a grant or donation received;
- a valuation of a property indicating a permanent diminution of value.

11.53 Where an event occurring subsequent to the year-end affects the amount or disclosure of an item in the financial statements this should be brought to the attention of the PCC with a view to the financial statements being amended.

Receipts & Payments basis

11.54 There is no specific requirement to consider events subsequent to the year-end, unless other examination procedures have given rise to concerns that need to be addressed in this way.

The PCC's annual report

11.55 Compare the financial statements to any financial references in the PCC's annual report, identify any major inconsistencies and consider the significance such matters will have on a proper and accurate understanding of the PCC's financial statements.

11.56 The PCC's annual report provides a report of the PCC's activities during the financial year. The Regulations specify the information that is to be contained in such reports. Guidance on this is given in Chapter 9.

11.57 Procedures should be directed at identifying inconsistencies with the financial statements which are misleading or which contradict the financial information contained in the financial statements.

11.58 Where inconsistencies are identified which may have a significant effect on the proper understanding of the financial statements, these should be drawn to the attention of the PCC. If no appropriate amendment is made to the annual report, then details of the matter should be provided in the examiner's report.

Examiner's report

11.59 Review and assess all conclusions drawn from the evidence obtained from the examination and consider the implications on the report to be made under the Church Regulations. If the examiner has cause to make a positive statement on any matter arising from his examination, then the examiner must ensure so far as is practicable that the report so made gives a clear explanation of the matter and of its financial effects on the financial statements presented.

11.60 The requirements as to the form and content of the examiner's report are set out in the Church Accounting Regulations 2006. Illustrative examples of such reports are included in Chapter 14. The examiner needs to consider carefully the conclusions drawn from the procedures undertaken in accordance with the Commission's directions, and the impact of these conclusions on the examiner's report.

11.61 In providing the examination report the examiner must state whether or not any matter has come to attention, in connection with the examination, which gives reasonable cause to believe that in any material respect:

- accounting records have not been kept in accordance with section 41 of the Charities Act 1993 and with the Church Accounting Regulations 2006;
- the financial statements do not accord with the accounting records; or
- whether financial statements which are prepared on the accruals basis fail to comply with regulations in respect of their form and content (other than the requirement to show a 'true and fair view').

11.62 Where any of the above concerns have been identified there should be a clear explanation of the nature of the failure and its financial effects on the financial statements. If the financial effects cannot be ascertained due to uncertainty, the nature of the uncertainty should be explained. If the concern relates to non-compliance with the Regulations as to the form and content of financial statements, this should be raised with the PCC to seek the necessary amendment to the financial statements.

11.63 The examiner is also required to state whether or not any matter has come to attention in connection with the examination to which, in the examiner's opinion, attention should be drawn in the report to enable a proper understanding of the financial statements to be reached. This is only likely to relate to significant matters.

11.64 Where such matters have come to attention, then they should be brought to the attention of the PCC with a view to seeking an amendment or adjustment to the financial statements. If concerns remain the matter should be addressed in the examiner's report. The matter concerned should be fully explained together with the financial effects on the financial statements.

11.65 There is also a requirement to provide a statement if the following matters have become apparent to the examiner during the course of the examination:

- any material expenditure or action which appears not to be in accordance within the objects of the PCC as set out in the PCCs (Powers) Measure 1956 or any special trusts of the PCC;
- the financial statements are inconsistent in any material respect with the annual report of the PCC;
- any failure to be provided with information and explanation by any past or present officer of the PCC that is considered necessary for the examination.

11.66 An understanding of the objectives and proper activities of the PCC should enable an examiner to recognize a material expenditure or action which does not appear to be in accordance with such objects. Whilst an immaterial technical breach would not concern the examiner, material actions or expenditure contrary to the objects of the PCC would be a major concern. The examiner need not carry out specific procedures to identify such breaches, but must include a statement on them in the report where they are identified.

11.67 Any failure to be provided with information and explanations may seriously hamper an examination. If significant information and explanations requested are not provided this matter must be included in the examiner's report.

11.68 Any major inconsistency between the financial statements and the PCC's annual report may give rise to misunderstanding. This should be brought to the attention of the PCC with a view to the amendment of the discrepancy. Where concerns still exist after any amendments are made this must be stated in the examiner's report.

Reports to the Charity Commission

11.69 If the examiner finds a problem that causes concern, s/he should be clear in his/her mind what the problem is. First s/he should clarify matters with the treasurer and, if appropriate, the minister and the churchwardens, who are the Bishop's Officers in the Parish. If the matter is legal or technical s/he should talk to an appropriate professional person and, if necessary, someone at the local diocesan office. If s/he is being obstructed in his/her work, for example not being given access to documents, s/he should contact the Archdeacon or diocesan office.

11.70 If, having established the problem, the examiner is still concerned, there are a number of alternative courses of action depending on the scale of the problem:

- The examiner can report the matter to the PCC separately, probably in the form of a letter – often called a 'management letter' when used by professional auditors. The letter will need to be carefully drafted to make it intelligible and tactful and it is good practice to discuss it with the treasurer and include their comments. The treasurer should ensure this is discussed at a PCC meeting. This would cover smaller concerns that the examiner might have, such as a poor or inefficient accounting system or areas where control is weak or, more likely, not clearly evidenced. Such a letter will help them improve their administration and control.
- The examiner may feel s/he has to make a qualified report attached to the financial statements. There may be an occasion where this is only a question of emphasis, for example where the PCC might be facing significant legal exposure from a court case which is yet to be resolved. Normally, however, a qualified report would be a serious matter and the independent examiner would be wise to seek advice from professional colleagues and the diocesan office before issuing the report. At the end of the day, however, it is for the examiner alone to determine what to say in his/her report and how to say it.
- The examiner may feel concerned that there are more serious problems – for example possible minor fraud or the inappropriate use of PCC funds (such as payment for a PCC Christmas dinner) – which need to be dealt with prior to considering issuing a report. These concerns should be raised with the minister and churchwardens. If the examiner finds that they are unwilling or unable to take action then s/he should consider exploring the problem with the Archdeacon responsible for the parish.
- At the most serious level this would be a matter that the independent examiner has to report to the Charity Commission under the Charities Act (see below). This covers circumstances where a charity has suffered serious loss or its assets are in serious danger (for example from embezzlement or inappropriate investment). This is dealt with below.

11.71 Inform the Charity Commissioners in writing if, whilst acting in the capacity of the examiner of a PCC, information or evidence is obtained which gives the examiner reasonable cause to believe that any one or more of the members of the PCC has been responsible for deliberate or reckless misconduct in the administration of the PCC.

11.72 The requirement to report such matters to the Charity Commission is contained in regulation 7(5) of the Charities (Accounts and Reports) Regulations 2005. If the examiner believes that one or more of the members of the PCC has been responsible for deliberate or reckless misconduct in the administration of a PCC then a separate written report of the matter must be forwarded to the Charity Commission. A reporting requirement would not arise through mere inadvertence or error of judgement on the part of a member whilst endeavouring honestly to carry out PCC duties. It is also unlikely that a reporting duty will arise unless a material loss or misapplication of funds has resulted or could result.

11.73 The duty to report relates to information or evidence obtained from the examiner's work undertaken in fulfilling the Regulations' directions or whilst acting in the capacity of the examiner of a PCC. It is not intended that the examiner should report on small or insignificant matters, particularly where such matters have been satisfactorily resolved internally.

11.74 The reporting duty relates primarily to the actions of the PCC. However, in considering individual actions, the examiner must take into account the members' overall responsibilities of management and control.

11.75 Where a reporting duty arises the examiner should provide details of the concern and, where possible, an estimate of the financial implications.

11.76 An independent examiner should ensure that the appropriate Archdeacon is copied in with any qualified or Charity Commission report. If the examiner suspects that a crime may have been committed (e.g. fraud) then, in conjunction with the Archdeacon, minister and churchwardens s/he should consider whether the matter should be reported to the police.

Audit/Independent examination comparison

Procedure/principle	Audit	Independent examination
Opinion required as to whether financial statements show a true and fair view.	Yes	No
Level of assurance given.	High, positive	Moderate, negative
Check accounting records to establish entitlement to independent examination instead of audit.	n/a	Yes
Obtain understanding of the PCC's organization, accounting system, activities and nature of its assets, liabilities, incoming resources and application of resources in order to plan appropriate procedures.	Yes	Yes
Record the procedures carried out and document matters that are important to support conclusions reached or statements provided in the report.	Yes	Yes
Consideration of accounting records.	(Companies Act): carry out procedures to enable formation of opinion as to whether accounting records have been maintained in accordance with s.221	Review with a view to identifying major failure to maintain accounting records in accordance with s.41 Charities Act 1993
Analytical review.	Yes	Yes
Substantive testing e.g. vouching source documents, physical inspection of fixed assets, obtaining bank confirmation of balances, inspection of investment certificates etc.	Yes	No – unless the analytical review shows unusual items for which the PCC cannot give satisfactory explanations.
Review financial statements for conformity with applicable rules on form and content.	Yes	Yes
Considering conformity with fundamental accounting concepts e.g. going concern. Consider any significant estimate or judgement made in preparing the financial statements.	Yes	Yes – in case of accruals-based accounts policies adopted by PCC should conform to fundamental accounting concepts and be appropriate to the activities of the PCC.
Post-balance sheet events.	Obtain sufficient appropriate evidence	Enquiry of PCC (accrual-based accounts)
Identify and report on any major inconsistencies between any financial references in the annual report and financial statements.	Yes	Yes
Obtain all information and explanations needed to carry out the scrutiny – report any failure.	Yes	Yes

Independent examination planning checklist

1. Is there any reason why I should not accept/continue with this appointment?

   Consider: – am I independent?
   - do I have the requisite ability and practical experience for a PCC of this complexity?
   - has my appointment been approved by the PCC and made by the APCM?
   - is the PCC aware of my responsibilities – possibly by signing and returning a letter of engagement?

2. Do the financial statements or accounting records confirm that the PCC's gross income and total expenditure is less than £250,000 in the current and two preceding years?

3. Are there any specific requirements for an audit to be carried out, for example, in any special trusts associated with the PCC or as a condition of any grants made to the PCC, that prevent me carrying out an independent examination?

4. For my first examination of this PCC, I have obtained background information on the PCC, how it is organized, the extent of its activities, the existence of parochial organizations and trusts and the nature of its income, expenditure, assets, liabilities and funds. For subsequent years, I have checked and updated the details from the previous year.

   These are set out on a separate sheet.

5. I have described in brief on a separate sheet the accounting records maintained by the PCC, which I have examined, and the key financial controls operated.

Name of independent examiner: Date:

Independent examination work programme

If any of the answers to these questions is 'no', full details of problems encountered and how they have been resolved should be included on a separate sheet.

	Financial statements	Completed satisfactorily YES	NO
1	Agree figures in the financial statements to the PCC's main accounting records (e.g. cash book).	❑	❑
2	Cross reference and attach to this programme a referenced set of financial statements and any supporting analysis necessary to show the link between the accounting records and the financial statements.	❑	❑
3	Read the PCC annual report and ensure it is consistent with both the financial statements and any other information gained during the course of the examination.	❑	❑
4	Consider if the PCC has adequately disclosed the transactions or interests that PCC members may have with it.	❑	❑

Completed satisfactorily

YES NO

Accounting records

5 Select a sample of entries from the main accounting records and trace them back to any supporting prime books that exist (e.g. cash book, petty cash book, planned giving register). ❑ ❑

6 Select a sample of entries from any of these prime books and trace them to the main accounting records. ❑ ❑

The items selected under 5 and 6 above should be recorded on a supporting working paper and the prime record to which they were checked or from which they were selected should be noted. These tests mirror each other but it is important that different items are selected for each test.

7 Test check the arithmetical accuracy of some of the accounting books and records. ❑ ❑

State on a separate sheet which records were checked and the sections covered by the checks.

Review of financial statements

8 Consider the PCC's incoming resources, resources expended, assets and liabilities as shown in the financial statements in the light of the general knowledge obtained about the PCC and its activities as well as budgets for the year and corresponding figures for the previous year. Where there are unexpected fluctuations or inconsistencies, obtain explanations from the PCC. ❑ ❑

9 Have any issues been identified which, whilst falling outside the scope of an independent examination, suggest that the financial statements are materially misstated? ❑ ❑

If 'Yes' include details on a separate sheet and state how they have been resolved.

10 Review minutes of PCC and other relevant committee meetings:

- identify major events, plans or decisions and changes in PCC officers and members and ensure they have been properly reflected in the accounting records, reports and financial statements;
- determine if the PCC has financed activities outside its objects and powers as outlined in the Guidance. ❑ ❑

11 Examine the year-end bank reconciliation (and, for more complex PCCs, any other control accounts) to ensure they do not include any unexpected or unusual items. ❑ ❑

Transaction testing

12 Select a sample of receipts and payments from the main accounting records and cross check the details to supporting invoices, vouchers or other similar documentation to ensure that the transactions are valid under the powers of the PCC. ❑ ❑

Note which transactions were examined on a separate sheet.

Reporting

13 Prepare a report to the PCC which is in accordance with CAR 2006. An example is provided within the Guidance. ❑ ❑

14 Matters identified during the course of the work which suggest legal, accounting or other similar problems should be carefully considered. If they represent significant instances of deliberate or reckless misconduct in the administration of the PCC, then a written report should be made to the Charity Commission and a copy provided to the archdeacon. ❑ ❑

		Completed satisfactorily	
	Additional work for financial statements prepared on the accruals basis	YES	NO
15	Review the accounting policies adopted by the PCC and ensure they are either the model policies provided in Chapter 8 or are consistent with the general Guidance.	❑	❑
16	Enquire if there have been any events since the year-end which should be disclosed in the financial statements or which indicate that amounts included in the financial statements should be amended.	❑	❑
17	Ensure any material contingencies or commitments identified have been properly shown in the financial statements.	❑	❑
18	Ensure the financial statements comply with the accounting and disclosure requirements of the Church Accounting Regulations 2006 and Guidance provided in Chapter 7 or 8.	❑	❑

Note: *This work programme should be suitable for most PCCs; however, where activities of the PCC are more complex and more judgemental issues are involved, the independent examiner should refer to guidance included in Chapter 10 of the Church's guidance to determine if additional or alternative procedures should be undertaken. These sheets may be copied.*

chapter 12

Glossary of terms

Accounting standards

Financial statements prepared on the accruals basis, which are intended to show a true and fair view, must conform to standards issued by the Accounting Standards Board or its predecessor, the Accounting Standards Committee. These standards, with which professional accountants are expected to be familiar, comprise a number of 'Statements of Standard Accounting Practice' (SSAP) and – more recently – 'Financial Reporting Standards' (FRS) and 'Urgent Issues Task Force abstracts' (UITF abstracts).

For financial statements on the accruals basis the notes should explain the accounting basis adopted to account for any **material** item in the financial statements. The following two notions are emphasized as having a pervasive role in financial statements and hence in the selection of accounting policies:

(1) the 'going concern' concept: i.e. the church is expected to continue in being, with much the same level of activity as at present;

(2) the 'accruals' concept: i.e. any revenues earned from the church's activities have been accounted for when they occur and have been matched with the costs incurred so that both are included in the same period of account.

Assets

Assets are the money, goods and property of the PCC, including any legal rights it may have to receive money, goods, services and property from others. 'Fixed assets' are assets which continue to be of value to the PCC year after year and which it holds on a long-term basis and therefore does not intend to dispose of in the short term. All other assets are regarded as 'current assets'.

The Church of England's consecrated lands and buildings and other benefice properties are not regarded as assets held by the PCC, and are therefore excluded from the annual financial statements altogether.

Furnishings, fittings and equipment (other than immovable items regarded as forming part of the building) for ecclesiastical use which are held by the churchwardens as custodian trustees and which the PCC has no power to dispose of without a faculty are regarded as inalienable assets. In such cases if a faculty is granted for the sale of a specific item, the realizable value of the asset in accordance with the terms of the faculty should then be included in the financial statements as an incoming resource represented by a current asset.

Investment assets are a separate category within fixed assets, except where the intention is to realize the asset without reinvestment of the sale proceeds. In such a case it should be reclassified as a current asset. Investment assets are generally held with the overall intention of retaining them long-term (as fixed assets) for the continuing benefit of the church in the form of income and capital appreciation.

Audit threshold

This is the threshold (which may include income, expenditure and asset limits) above which a charity will be required to have a statutory audit.

Branches

Branches is the word used in the SORP to describe entities or administrative bodies which conduct a particular aspect of a charity's work. They may or may not be separate legal entities, but they may be either part of the charity or special trusts under Part VI of the Charities Act 1993. They must be accounted for within the financial statements of the main charity. District churches within an ecclesiastical parish, for example, would be accounted for either as branches or as special trusts in the PCC financial statements, as would also the Men's Fellowship and the Mothers' and Toddlers' Group.

Capital – endowment

The **capital** (i.e. endowment) of a church is a class of restricted fund (or funds) which the PCC must retain for the benefit of the church and not spend. As such, it must be retained either in the form of assets for use by the church or in the form of investments producing an income. For charity law purposes, it is called 'permanent endowment' if it must not be spent at all (i.e. where the PCC has no express or implied legal power to convert it into income). However 'expendable endowment' is a form of endowment capital where it does have such a power, which the PCC can use or not use at its own discretion. Expendable endowment is that part of an endowed fund which has not yet been converted into income by the exercise of the power to do so by the PCC.

'Capital funds' must by law be administered separately from 'income funds', and the annual financial statements should therefore maintain strict distinction between them.

Connected charities

A charity is connected with the PCC if it has common, parallel or related objects and activities and either common control or unity of administration.

So that the reader can gain a full appreciation of the scope of the activities of the PCC, the financial statements should also provide information on the charities that are connected with it. It will be sufficient to note the name of the connected charity, the areas (i.e. activity and/or location) in which it operates and how the reader can contact it.

Consolidation and aggregation

There has been a tendency for the word **consolidation** to be used in places where it is not appropriate.

Branches and special trusts of a charity must be accounted for by the charity of which they form part. In the charity's own statutory accounts under charity law, all its parts are **aggregated** in such a way as to distinguish the terms of trust on which the charity's various funds are held. This is not at all the same as 'consolidated accounts', which are prepared from, and in addition to, the individual statutory accounts of a 'parent undertaking' and the 'subsidiary undertakings' under its control as required by company law. Consolidated accounts are not yet a statutory requirement of charity law, but the Charities SORP recommends them where appropriate in order to show a true and fair view of the group as a whole.

Contingency

A **contingency** is a condition which exists at the balance sheet date, where the outcome will be confirmed only on the occurrence or non-occurrence of one or more uncertain future events.

Custodian trustee

Custodian trustee means any person or body appointed to have the guardianship, as distinct from the management, of property on behalf of another charity whose trustees have general control and management and are accountable for it in law. The term includes for present purposes any other non-executive trustee. For example, the PCC is accountable as managing trustees for church property held by the Diocesan Board of Finance as custodian trustees on its behalf.

Designated fund

If the PCC sets aside part of its unrestricted funds for a particular project it may place these in a separate unrestricted fund called a **designated fund.** Funds so designated may be redesignated by the PCC and so designation does not prevent funds being spent on any other purposes. All unrestricted funds comprise income funds which the PCC must spend within a reasonable time.

Endowment fund

(See **Capital** above.)

Fund

A **fund** is a pool of unexpended resources comprising money and other assets held in trust by the PCC. It may be an **unrestricted fund** to be spent on general purposes (in which case it must be an 'income fund'), or it may be a **restricted fund.** The restricted fund will be either a capital (endowment) fund or an income fund, depending on the nature of the restriction. Where the fund is held on trust for spending on specified purposes, it is known as a 'restricted income fund'.

Fund-raising costs

Fund-raising and publicity costs include:

- Costs of generating voluntary income which are amounts spent or payments made, by a charity or its agent, to encourage others to make voluntary contributions to the church, such as the costs of some forms of Christian Stewardship programme. When fund-raising for a particular project such costs will include payments made for advertising and direct mail materials, as well as any payments to an agent acting as fund raiser on the PCC's behalf.
- Fund-raising trading costs including cost of goods sold and other costs associated with the trading operation.

Income

All money and other assets held on trust for spending in furtherance of the PCC's objects within a reasonable time of receipt belong to its income funds, whereas money and other assets held on trust for retention belong to its capital (endowment) funds (see above). The annual financial statements should therefore maintain strict distinction between income funds and capital (endowment) funds. Thus gains arising on disposal or revaluation of investments and fixed assets used by the PCC must be accounted for as accruing to the fund of which the asset itself forms part.

Gross income

Gross income is a term used in the Charities Act 1993 to determine the thresholds made by the Act and Regulations. The gross income of the PCC excludes unrealised gains and includes any amounts of expendable endowment converted into income.

Liabilities

A **liability** is an obligation of an entity to transfer economic benefits which:

(a) is expected to be settled by the entity parting with assets or in some way losing an economic benefit; and

(b) results from past transactions or events; and

(c) embodies a present duty or responsibility to one or more other entities that entails settlement at a specified or determinable future date, on the occurrence of a specified event, or on demand; and

(d) results from a duty or responsibility which obligates the entity either legally, or practically (a constructive obligation), because it would be financially or otherwise operationally damaging to the entity not to discharge the duty or responsibility.

A moral obligation – such as results from the making of a non-contractual promise – does not create a liability unless it meets the definition above.

Market value

Market value is the price at which an asset could be, or could be expected to be, sold or acquired in a public market between a willing buyer and willing seller.

Material

An item is **material** if, taking all the circumstances into account, its inclusion (or exclusion) would be likely to influence the reader of the report and financial statements in relation to the report and financial statements as a whole or in relation to the context of which the item forms part. The PCC is responsible for deciding whether an item is or is not material. In cases of doubt an item should be treated as material.

Receipts & Payments account

The **Receipts & Payments** account recognizes only money received and paid in the year and excludes the value of all other assets received in kind (goods for sale or distribution, debts, investments, equipment, properties, etc.) unless and until converted into money. A list of any such assets retained at the year-end should be provided in the statement of assets and liabilities.

Records

The Charities Act 1993 requires all charities to maintain proper accounting records and specifically to include a record of assets and liabilities as well as receipts and payments. The Act says that the accounting records must be such as to enable financial statements which comply with the Regulations to be prepared if that is what is required.

Related parties

Related parties include all of the following:

(a) any charity trustee and custodian trustee of the charity;

(b) any person or body with:

(i) *either* the power to appoint or remove a significant proportion of the charity trustees of the charity. All or a majority of the trustees should always be treated as a "significant proportion". Fewer than 50% of the trustees may be a "significant proportion" if they collectively have a dominant influence on the operation of the charity, as, for example, is likely to be the case if one body has the power to appoint/remove 7 of a body of 15 trustees, and 8 other different bodies had the right to appoint/remove 1 each,

(ii) *or* whose consent is required to the exercise of any of the discretions of those trustees,

(iii) *or* who is entitled to give directions to those trustees as to the exercise of any of those discretions;

(c) any institution connected with the charity, and any director of such an institution. An institution is connected with a charity if *either*:

(i) it is controlled by (in Scotland managed or controlled by) the charity. "Controlled" means that the charity is able to secure that the affairs of the institution are conducted in accordance with its wishes. A charity will control another if it is trustee of that charity or has power to appoint or remove a significant proportion of its trustees. *or*

(ii) a participating interest in it is beneficially owned by the charity. "Participating interest" means that the charity:

(a) is interested in shares comprised in the equity share capital of the body of a nominal value of more than one-fifth of that share capital; or

(b) is entitled to exercise or control the exercise of more than one-fifth of the voting power at any general meeting of that body;

(d) any other charity with which it is commonly controlled. Common control exists if:

(i) the same person, or persons have the right to appoint a majority of the charity trustees of both or all the charities; or

(ii) the same person, or persons, hold a majority of the voting rights in the administration of both or all of the charities.

Persons who are related with each other through family or business relationships should be treated as the same person for the present purposes.

A charity is not necessarily related to another charity simply because a particular person happens to be a trustee of both. It will only be related if one charity subordinates its interests to the other charity in any transaction because of this relationship;

(e) any pension fund for the benefit of:

(i) the employees of the charity, and/or

(ii) of any other person who is a related party of the charity;

(f) any officer, agent or employee of the charity having authority or responsibility for directing or controlling the major activities or resources of the charity; and

(g) any person connected to a person who is related to the charity including:

(i) members of the same family or household of the charity trustee or related person who may be expected to influence, or be influenced by, that person in their dealings with the charity;

(ii) the trustees of any trust, not being a charity, the beneficiaries or potential beneficiaries of which include a charity trustee or related person or a person referred to in (i) as being connected with a charity trustee or to a related person, as the case may be;

(iii) any business partner of a charity trustee or related person, or of any person referred to in (i) or (ii) as being connected with a charity trustee or to a related person, as the case may be;

(iv) any body corporate, not being a company which is controlled entirely by one or more charitable institutions, in which:

(a) the charity trustee has, or the charity trustee and any other charity trustee or trustees or person or persons referred to in (i), (ii) or (iii) above as being connected with a charity trustee, taken together, have a participating interest; or

(b) the related person has, or the related person and any other related parties of the charity, taken together, have a participating interest;

(v) Any person or body who makes available to the charity the services of any person or body as a charity trustee is connected with a charity trustee.

Reserves

The term "reserves" has a variety of technical and ordinary meanings, depending on the context in which it is used. In the SORP the term "reserves" (unless otherwise indicated) is used to describe that part of a PCC's income funds that is freely available.

This definition of **reserves** therefore normally excludes:

- permanent endowment;
- expendable endowment;
- restricted funds;

and any part of unrestricted funds not readily available for spending, specifically:

- income funds which could only be realised by disposing of fixed assets held for charity use and programme related investments.

Individual charities may have more or less reserves available to them than this simple calculation suggests, for example:

(a) Expendable endowments may be readily available for spending; or

(b) Unrestricted funds may be earmarked or designated for essential future spending and reduce the amount readily available.

For further information, see the Charity Commission's publication CC19 on Charities' Reserves.

Resources expended

Resources expended means all costs, as recorded, which have been incurred in the course of expending or utilizing the PCC's funds.

For financial statements prepared on the accruals basis, this includes all claims against the PCC upon being recognized as liabilities by the PCC, as well as all accruals and payments made by the PCC and all losses on the disposal of fixed assets together with all provisions for permanent diminution in value of any tangible fixed assets.

For all the purposes of the Charities Act 1993, however, when determining the size of the PCC by reference to its 'total expenditure' any losses on disposal of investments and fixed assets used by the PCC are disregarded.

Restricted fund

A **restricted fund** is a fund subject to specific trusts (e.g. by a letter from the donor at the time of gift, or by the terms of a public appeal). It may be a capital fund, which cannot be spent but must be retained for the benefit of the Church, or it may be an income fund, which must be spent on the specified purpose(s) within a reasonable time.

Sales of investments and other assets

The proceeds of **sale of an investment or other asset** form part of the fund to which the asset belonged. In order to ensure that the money goes to the correct fund it is essential to know to which fund each asset and liability belongs. This information should therefore be noted in the statement of assets and liabilities.

Trading

In a strict legal sense trading activities are those carried out under contract whether at the point of sale or otherwise, where goods and services are provided in return for consideration for those goods or services. Normally trading activities are carried out on a regular basis with a view to making profits, though it is possible that some one-off activities could be regarded as trading.

However, in an economic sense, trading can be regarded as the provision of goods and services in return for a payment whether or not this payment is in fact under contract. Therefore, certain incoming grants which are in a legal sense donations, but which have specific terms attached to them such that a charity becomes entitled to the payment on the provision of specified goods or services, are in the context of the SORP regarded as trading income. This is because the charity has an obligation to provide the specific services or goods in the same way that it would have to provide them under contract. If it fails to provide the goods or services then if the funds are by way of grant this will be a breach of trust but if they are by way of contract this will be by way of breach of contract. The legal remedies of the funding body are different depending upon the circumstances.

Similarly the sale of donated goods is in a legal sense regarded as the realization of a donation. However, in the context of this SORP it is regarded as trading, and recognized as an activity for generating funds because it is so similar to the sale of bought-in goods as to be indistinguishable in the actual processes involved except for the legal distinction.

For income tax, corporation tax and VAT purposes trading must be interpreted within the meaning of the legislation governing those taxes.

Unrestricted fund

All funds held for general purposes are known as **unrestricted funds** to distinguish them from **restricted funds** (see above). The Church's unrestricted funds are therefore those which are held for spending at the PCC's discretion. These include any further funds which the PCC has designated for particular purposes (see **designated fund**).

chapter 13

Extracts from related legislation

The following are extracts from legislation that are referred to above in this publication.

Church Accounting Regulations 2006

Made (approved by the General Synod) 8 July 2006

Coming into force 1 August 2006

In pursuance of the power conferred by rule 54(8) of the Church Representation Rules the following Regulations are hereby prescribed by the Business Committee of the General Synod:

Definitions

1. In these Regulations:

   'the Act' means the Charities Act 1993;

   'the Charity Commission' means the Charity Commissioners for England and Wales;

   'Council' means the parochial church council of a parish; and

   'the SORP' means the Statement of Recommended Practice for accounting and reporting by charities published by the Charity Commission on 4 March 2005 as from time to time amended, and any replacement Statement of Recommended Practice for accounting and reporting by charities published by the Charity Commission.

Revocation of the Church Accounting Regulations 1997 to 2001

2. The Church Accounting Regulations 1997 to 2001 shall continue to have effect in relation to accounts and annual reports of a Council for financial years ending on or before 31 December but, subject thereto, are hereby revoked.

Requirements in relation to accounts, audit, etc.

3. Subject to Regulation 4, a Council shall comply with its obligations under the Act (including any regulations made thereunder) and under the SORP with regard to:

   (a) the keeping of accounting records for the Council;
   (b) the preparation and preservation of annual statements of account for the Council;
   (c) the auditing or independent examination of the statements of account of the Council;
   (d) the transmission of the statements of account of the Council to the Charity Commission;
   (e) the preparation of an annual report for the Council and its transmission to the Charity Commission; and
   (f) the preparation of an annual return for the Council and its transmission to the Charity Commission.

4. If, in respect of a financial year of the Council, the accounts of the Council are not otherwise required by the Act to be audited or examined by an independent examiner, the accounts of the Council for that year shall be examined by an independent examiner; and such examination shall be conducted, and treated for all purposes, as if it were an examination required by the Act.

Commencement and citation

5. (1) These Regulations shall come into force on the 1 August 2006 so as to have effect in relation to accounts and annual reports of a Council for financial years ending on or after 31 December 2006.

(2) These regulations may be cited as the Church Accounting Regulations 2006..

Parochial Church Councils (Powers) Measure 1956

1 Definitions

In this Measure:

'Council' means a parochial church council;

'Diocesan Authority' means the Diocesan Board of Finance or any existing or future body appointed by the Diocesan Synod to act as trustees of diocesan trust property;

'Minister' and 'Parish' have the meanings respectively assigned to them in the Rules for the Representation of the Laity.

2 General functions of council

(1) It shall be the duty of the minister and the parochial church council to consult together on matters of general concern and importance to the parish.

(2) The functions of parochial church councils shall include:

(a) cooperation with the minister in promoting in the parish the whole mission of the Church, pastoral, evangelistic, social and ecumenical;
(b) the consideration and discussions of matters concerning the Church of England or any other matters of religious or public interest, but not the declaration of the doctrine of the Church on any question;
(c) making known and putting into effect any provision made by the diocesan synod or the deanery synod, but without prejudice to the powers of the council on any particular matter;
(d) giving advice to the diocesan synod and the deanery synod on any matter referred to the council;
(e) raising such matters as the council consider appropriate with the diocesan synod or deanery synod.

(3) In the exercise of its functions the parochial church council shall take into consideration any expression of opinion by any parochial church meeting.

3 Council to be body corporate

Every council shall be a body corporate by the name of the parochial church council of the parish for which it is appointed and shall have perpetual succession. Any act of the council may be signified by an instrument executed pursuant to a resolution of the council and under the hands or if an instrument under seal is required under the hands and seals of the chairman presiding and two other members of the council present at the meeting at which such resolution is passed.

7 Miscellaneous powers of council

The council of every parish shall have the following powers in addition to any powers conferred by the Constitution or otherwise by this Measure:–

(i) power to frame an annual budget of moneys required for the maintenance of the work of the Church in the parish and otherwise and to take such steps as they think necessary for the raising collecting and allocating of such moneys;

(ii) power to make levy and collect a voluntary church rate for any purpose connected with the affairs of the church including the administrative expenses of the council and the costs of any legal proceedings;

(iii) power jointly with the minister to appoint and dismiss the parish clerk and sexton or any persons performing or assisting to perform the duties of parish clerk or sexton and to determine their salaries and the conditions of the tenure of their offices or of their employment but subject to the rights of any persons holding the said offices at the appointed day;

(iv) power jointly with the minister to determine the objects to which all moneys to be given or collected in church shall be allocated;

(v) power to make representations to the bishop with regard to any matter affecting the welfare of the church in the parish.

8 Financial statements of the council

(1) Every council shall furnish to the annual parochial church meeting for discussion the financial statements of the council for the financial year immediately preceding the meeting.

(2) The financial year referred to in subsection (1) above shall be such period as may be prescribed and the financial statements referred to in that subsection shall be prepared in the prescribed form, audited or independently examined as prescribed and published and displayed in the prescribed manner.

(3) In subsection (2) above 'prescribed' means prescribed by the Church Representation Rules or by regulations made under those Rules.

The Charities Act 1993: Part VI
Charity Accounts, reports and returns

Duty to keep accounting records

41. (1) The charity trustees of a charity shall ensure that accounting records are kept in respect of the charity which are sufficient to show and explain all the charity's transactions, and which are such as to–

(a) disclose at any time, with reasonable accuracy, the financial position of the charity at that time, and

(b) enable the trustees to ensure that, where any statements of accounts are prepared by them under section 42(1) below, those statements of accounts comply with the requirements of regulations under that provision.

(2) The accounting records shall in particular contain–

(a) entries showing from day to day all sums of money received and expended by the charity, and the matters in respect of which the receipt and expenditure takes place; and

(b) a record of the assets and liabilities of the charity.

(3) The charity trustees of a charity shall preserve any accounting records made for the purposes of this section in respect of the charity for at least six years from the end of the financial year of the charity in which they are made.

(4) Where a charity ceases to exist within the period of six years mentioned in subsection (3) above as it applies to any accounting records, the obligation to preserve those records in accordance with that subsection shall continue to be discharged by the last charity trustees of the charity, unless the Commissioners consent in writing to the records being destroyed or otherwise disposed of.

Annual statements of accounts

42. (1) The charity trustees of a charity shall (subject to subsection (3) below) prepare in respect of each financial year of the charity a statement of accounts complying with such requirements as to its form and contents as may be prescribed by regulations made by the Secretary of State.

(2) Without prejudice to the generality of subsection (1) above, regulations under that subsection may make provision–

(a) for any such statement to be prepared in accordance with such methods and principles as are specified or referred to in the regulations;
(b) as to any information to be provided by way of notes to the accounts;

and regulations under that subsection may also make provision for determining the financial years of a charity for the purposes of this Act and any regulations made under it.

(3) Where a charity's gross income in any financial year does not exceed £100,000, the charity trustees may, in respect of that year, elect to prepare the following, namely–

(a) a R&P account, and
(b) a statement of assets and liabilities,

instead of a statement of accounts under subsection (1) above.

(4) The charity trustees of a charity shall preserve–

(a) any statement of accounts prepared by them under subsection (1) above, or
(b) any account and statement prepared by them under subsection (3) above,

for at least six years from the end of the financial year to which any such statement relates or (as the case may be) to which any such account and statement relate.

(5) Subsection (4) of section 41 above shall apply in relation to the preservation of any such statement or account and statement as it applies in relation to the preservation of any accounting records (the references to subsection (3) of that section being read as references to subsection (4) above).

(6) The Secretary of State may by order amend subsection (3) above by substituting a different sum for the sum for the time being specified there.

Annual audit or examination of charity accounts

43. (1) Subsection (2) below applies to a financial year of a charity ('the relevant year') if the charity's gross income or total expenditure in any of the following, namely–

(a) the relevant year,
(b) the financial year of the charity immediately preceding the relevant year (if any), and
(c) the financial year of the charity immediately preceding the year specified in paragraph (b) above (if any),

exceeds £250,000.

(2) If this subsection applies to a financial year of a charity, the accounts of the charity for that year shall be audited by a person who–

(a) is, in accordance with section 25 of the Companies Act 1989 (eligibility for appointment), eligible for appointment as a company auditor, or
(b) is a member of a body for the time being specified in regulations under section 44 below and is under the rules of that body eligible for appointment as auditor of the charity.

(3) If subsection (2) above does not apply to a financial year of a charity and its gross income or total expenditure in that year exceeds £10,000 then (subject to subsection (4) below) the accounts of the charity for that year shall, at the election of the charity trustees, either–

(a) be examined by an independent examiner, that is to say an independent person who is reasonably believed by the trustees to have the requisite ability and practical experience to carry out a competent examination of the accounts, or
(b) be audited by such a person as is mentioned in subsection (2) above.

The Charities (Accounts and Reports) Regulations 2005

Form and content of statement of accounts

3. (3) The requirements as to form and content of a statement of accounts to which this regulation applies are those set out in the following provisions of this regulation.

(4) The statement shall consist of–

(a) a statement of financial activities which shall show the total incoming resources and application of the resources, together with any other movements in the total resources, of the charity during the financial year in respect of which the statement is prepared; and

(b) a balance sheet which shall show the state of affairs of the charity as at the end of the financial year in respect of which the statement is prepared.

(5) The statement shall be prepared in accordance with the following principles, namely that–

(a) the statement of financial activities shall give a true and fair view of the incoming resources and application of the resources of the charity in the financial year in respect of which the statement is prepared;

(b) the balance sheet shall give a true and fair view of the state of affairs of the charity at the end of that year;

(c) where compliance with the following requirements of this regulation would not be sufficient to give a true and fair view, the necessary additional information shall be given in the statement of accounts or in notes to the accounts;

(d) if in special circumstances compliance with any of those requirements would be inconsistent with giving a true and fair view, the charity trustees shall depart from the requirement to the extent necessary to give a true and fair view.

(6) The statement–

(a) shall be prepared in accordance with the methods and principles set out in the SORP; and

(b) subject to the following three paragraphs of this regulation, shall, with respect to any amount required to be shown in the statement of financial activities or in the balance sheet, also show the corresponding amount for the financial year immediately preceding that to which the statement or balance sheet relates.

(7) Where that corresponding amount is not comparable with the amount to be shown for the item in question in respect of the financial year to which the statement of financial activities or balance sheet relates, the former amount shall be adjusted.

(8) Where in the financial year to which the statement of accounts relates the effect of paragraph (5) and paragraph (6)(a) above is that there is nothing required to be shown in respect of a particular item, but an amount was required to be shown in respect of that item in the statement of accounts for the immediately preceding financial year, those provisions shall have effect as if such an amount were required to be shown in the statement of accounts in the financial year to which the statement relates, and that amount were nil.

(9) Where a charity has more than one fund, only amounts corresponding to the entries in the statement of financial activities relating to the totals of both or all of the funds of the charity need be shown.

(10) There shall be provided by way of notes to the accounts the information specified in Schedule 1 to these Regulations.

(11) The balance sheet shall be signed by one or more of the charity trustees of the charity, each of whom has been authorized to do so, and shall specify the date on which the statement of accounts of which the balance sheet forms part was approved by the charity trustees.

Church Representation Rules

Parochial Church Meetings and Councils

Business

9. (1) The annual meeting shall receive from the parochial church council and shall be free to discuss–

(a) a report on changes in the roll since the last annual parochial church meeting or, in a year in which a new roll is prepared, a report on the numbers entered on the new roll;
(b) an annual report on the proceedings of the parochial church council and the activities of the parish generally;
(c) the financial statements of the parochial church council for the year ending on the 31st December immediately preceding the meeting, independently examined or audited as provided by paragraph (3) hereof;
(d) a report upon the fabric, goods and ornaments of the church or churches of the parish under section 5 of the Care of Churches and Ecclesiastical Jurisdiction Measure 1991; and
(e) a report on the proceedings of the deanery synod.

(2) The council shall cause a copy of the said roll to be available for inspection at the meeting.

(3) The said financial statements shall–

(a) be independently examined or audited in such manner as shall be prescribed in accordance with rule 54(8);
(b) be considered and, if thought fit, approved by the parochial church council and signed by the chairman presiding at the meeting of the council; and
(c) be displayed for a continuous period of at least seven days before the annual meeting, including at least one Sunday when the church is used for worship, on a notice-board either inside or outside the church.

(4) The annual report referred to in paragraph (1)(b) above and the said financial statements shall be prepared in such form as shall be prescribed in accordance with rule 54(8) hereof for consideration by the annual meeting. Following such meeting the council shall cause copies of the annual report and statements to be sent within twenty-eight days of the annual meeting to the secretary of the diocesan board of finance for retention by the board.

(5) The annual meeting shall in the manner provided by rule 11–

(a) elect in every third year parochial representatives of the laity to the deanery synod;
(b) elect parochial representatives of the laity to the parochial church council;
(c) appoint sidesmen;
(d) appoint the independent examiner or auditor to the council for a term of office ending at the close of the next annual meeting, provided that such person shall not be a member of the council;

and the elections and appointments shall be carried out in the above order.

Supplementary and interpretation

54. (8) (a) In these rules any matters or regulations to be prescribed shall be prescribed by the Business Committee of the General Synod in accordance with the following procedure.

(b) Any matters or regulations made under this rule shall be laid before the General Synod and shall not come into force until they have been approved by the General Synod, whether with or without amendment.

(c) Where the Business Committee determines that matters or regulations made under this rule do not need to be debated by the General Synod then, unless–

(i) notice is given by a member of the General Synod in accordance with Standing Orders that he wishes the business to be debated, or

(ii) notice is so given by any such member that he wishes to move an amendment to the business,

the matters or regulations shall for the proposes of sub-paragraph (b) above be deemed to have been approved by the General Synod without amendment.

General provisions relating to parochial church councils

Officers of the Council

1. (g) If an independent examiner or auditor to the council is not appointed by the annual meeting or if an independent examiner or auditor appointed by the annual meeting is unable or unwilling to act, an independent examiner or auditor (who shall not be a member of the council) shall be appointed by the council for a term of office ending at the close of the next annual meeting. The remuneration (if any) of the independent examiner or auditor shall be paid by the council.

Minutes

12. (e) The independent examiner or auditor of the council's financial statements, the bishop, the archdeacon and any person authorized by one of them in writing shall have access to the approved minutes of the council meetings without the authority of the council.

chapter 14

Practical examples

14.1 This chapter contains an example of each of the following:

- An annual report taking advantage of relaxations for small charities
- A Receipts & Payments account and statement of assets and liabilities (including notes)
- A Receipts & Payments account using columnar basis
- Accruals accounts, comprising SOFA, balance sheet and notes
- A balance sheet on a columnar basis
- An independent examiner's report
- A letter setting out agreed Terms of Engagement for the independent examiner

EXAMPLE: Annual report taking advantage of relaxations for small charities

St Emilion's Church, Barhester – Annual Report of the Parochial Church Council for the Year Ended 31 December 2006

Administrative information

St Emilion's Church is situated in The Green, Barchester. It is part of the Diocese of Salisbury within the Church of England. The correspondence address is The Vicarage, Church Street, Barchester.

The Parochial Church Council (PCC) is a charity excepted from registration with the Charity Commission.

PCC members who have served from 1 January 2006 until the date this report was approved are:

Incumbent:	The Revd Onesimus Og	Chairman
Reader:	Mr Adam Agrippa	
Wardens:	Mrs Bathsheba Babylon	
	Mr Caleb Cornelius	Vice chairman
Representatives on the Deanery Synod:	Mr David Dathan	
	Mr Eli Emmaus	Secretary
	Mr Felix Festus	
Elected members:	Miss Gomer Goliath	(From APCM 2006 – 5 April 2006)
	Mrs Hannah Hosea	Treasurer
	Mr Ishmael Isaiah	
	Miss Jemima Joshua	
	Mrs Kezia Korah	
	Miss Leah Lot	(Until APCM 2006 – 5 April 2006)
	Mr Mark Moses	
	Miss Naomi Noah	
	Mr Paul Potiphar	(Until APCM 2006 – 5 April 2006)

Miss Ruth Reuben
Mr Timothy Thomas (From APCM 2006 – 5 April 2006)

Structure, governance and management

The method of appointment of PCC members is set out in the Church Representation Rules. All Church attendees are encouraged to register on the Electoral Roll and stand for election to the PCC.

Objectives and activities

St Emilion's PCC has the responsibility of co-operating with the incumbent, the Revd Onesimus Og, in promoting in the ecclesiastical parish the whole mission of the Church, pastoral, evangelistic, social and ecumenical. It also has maintenance responsibilities for the Church Centre complex of St Emilion's, The Green, Barchester.

Achievements and performance

Church attendance

There are 273 parishioners on the Church Electoral Roll, 91 of whom are not resident within the parish. 18 names were added during the year and 9 were removed either through death or because they moved away from the parish. The average weekly attendance, counted during October, was 207, but this number increased at festivals and two Christmas carol services had to be held to seat all those who wished to attend.

Review of the year

The full PCC met six times during the year with an average level of attendance of 80 per cent. Committees met between meetings and minutes of their deliberations were received by the full PCC and discussed where necessary.

A great deal of time and thought was spent during the year on making best use of the new services. Many have said how much easier it is to follow the services now that they are printed out in booklets. We also agreed the new style of family worship on the morning of the 3rd Sunday each month. This has meant that special arrangements have had to be made for baptisms and for welcoming the families at corporate worship on the 1st Sunday of each month. It is pleasing to be able to report that the new arrangements have been well received since they came into operation during September. They will be reviewed by the PCC after 12 months.

The PCC has also focused its attention on the questions posed to parishes in the deanery about the most effective deployment of stipendiary and non-stipendiary clergy.

The kitchen in the church hall was refurbished during August and the new environment meets the stringent health and safety requirements and allows us to continue the old people's luncheon club on Saturdays. A new photocopier was purchased.

The Mission and Evangelism Committee is to be congratulated on its fund-raising efforts. £1,350 was raised for the Southern Africa Famine appeal. It is good that these efforts on behalf of others can be combined with opportunities for fellowship.

The planned giving through envelopes and banker's orders increased by 8 per cent and it was good to see the use of Gift Aid envelopes increased. However, the total income, including tax recovered but excluding the legacy, went up by only 2 per cent owing to a reduction in general donations and because no rummage sales were held. We were grateful for a pecuniary legacy of £1,000 from the estate of Mrs Esther Ruth. £2,000 was set aside towards the cost of the much-needed cleaning of the organ. The work was completed in time for Christmas.

The state of the nave roof has been causing concern for some time. After many years, during which routine maintenance has been carried out, a detailed report on its condition will be prepared by the architect at the next routine inspection in April 2007. We have already anticipated the need for major structural renewal, and it is our policy to make provisions from general income in the hope that an urgent appeal can be avoided.

Financial review

Total receipts on ordinary unrestricted funds were £63,450 and are detailed in the financial statements. The freehold house at 36 Church Road continues to be let temporarily, which provided a gross income of £3,700.

£60,850 was spent to provide the Christian ministry from St Emilion's Church, including the contribution to the diocesan parish share, which largely provides the stipends and housing for the clergy. It increased by 12 per cent. The sum that the churches in the deanery have to find is shared between the churches according to a formula that is based mainly on a head count of the congregations. We have to find more of the sum at St Emilion's as the size of our congregation increased more compared with other churches.

The net result for the year was an excess of receipts over payments of £2,600. After transferring £2,000 to the designated Organ fund to cover expenditure incurred towards the end of the year (paid in 2007), and adding bank and deposit balances brought forward at the beginning of the year, the balances carried forward at 31 December for unrestricted funds totalled £4,900.

Reserves policy

It is PCC policy to maintain a balance on unrestricted funds (if possible), which equates to approximately six months' unrestricted payments, to cover emergency situations that may arise from time to time. The balance of £4,900 on unrestricted funds at the year-end did not match this target.

The balance of £17,050 in the Fabric restricted fund is retained towards meeting the cost of the nave roof repairs detailed above.

It is our policy to invest our funds balances with the CBF Church of England Deposit Fund.

Approved by the PCC on 8 March 2007 and signed on their behalf by Revd Onesimus Og (PCC chairman).

EXAMPLE: Receipts & Payments Account and Statement of Assets and Liabilities (including notes)

St Emilion's Church, Barchester – Financial Statements for the Year ended 31 December 2006

	2006		2005	
	£	£	£	£
General (Unrestricted) Fund Receipts & Payments Account				
Receipts				
Voluntary Receipts				
Regular Giving				
Planned giving	29,400		27,200	
Collections and other giving	9,900		10,600	
Income tax recovered	8,700	48,000	8,300	46,100
Other voluntary receipts				
Legacy	1,000		–	
Donations	1,700	2,700	1,800	1,800
Receipts from activities for generating funds				
Parish magazine – sales and adverts	2,200		2,100	
Rent from temporary letting of Curate's House	3,700		3,700	
Summer Fete and Christmas Bazaar	2,400		2,500	
Rummage sales	–	8,300	700	9,000
Receipts from Church activities				
Fees	400		300	
Contributions for local community use of Church Centre	3,900	4,300	3,800	4,100
Receipts from investments				
Bank and CBF Deposit account interest	150		200	
Dividend on CBF Church of England Investment Fund	500	650	500	700
Total Receipts		**63,950**		**61,700**
Payments				
Church activities				
Overseas mission and relief agencies	2,550		2,550	
Diocesan parish share	41,500		37,050	
Church running expenses	5,200		5,300	
Clergy expenses	1,900		1,800	
Cost of services	2,600		2,100	
Buildings maintenance	2,500		5,200	
Printing the Magazine	1,800		1,800	
Printing and stationery	1,100		1,200	
Cleaning Church Centre	1,200		1,200	
Training course – Sunday school teachers	1,000		–	
Total Payments		**61,350**		**58,200**
Excess of Receipts over Payments		**2,600**		**3,500**
Transfer to Designated organ fund		2,000		–
		600		3,500
Bank current and deposit accounts at 1 January		4,300		800
Bank current and deposit accounts at 31 December		4,900		4,300

Church Fabric (including Tower) Receipts & Payments account – Restricted fund

	2006		2005	
	£	£	£	£
Receipts				
Restricted donations	4,100		5,250	
Interest from CBF Deposit fund	950	5,050	700	5,950
Payments				
Repairs to the lych-gate roof		1,400		–
Excess of receipts over payments		**3,650**		**5,950**
Bank current and deposit accounts at 1 January		13,400		7,450
Bank current and deposit accounts at 31 December		17,050		13,400

Church flowers – Restricted fund

		2006	2005
Receipts	Donations	350	–
Payments	Purchase of Easter lilies	350	–

Organ fund Receipts & Payments account – Designated fund

		2006	2005
Receipts	Interest from CBF Deposit Fund	250	200
Payments	Organ inspection	–	150
Excess of receipts over payments		**250**	**50**
Transfers	from general fund	2,000	–
		2,250	50
Bank current and deposit accounts at 1 January		3,300	3,250
Bank current and deposit accounts at 31 December		5,550	3,300

Statement of Assets and Liabilities at 31 December 2006

	2006	2005
	£	£
Cash funds		
Bank current account	400	350
CBF Deposit fund	27,100	20,650
Total bank current and deposit accounts	27,500	21,000

(£4,900 unrestricted, £17,050 restricted Fabric fund, £5,550 designated Organ fund)

	2006	2005
Other monetary assets (all in respect of unrestricted funds)		
Local Authority grant for churchyard	300	–
End of year income tax claim (recd Jan 2007)	2,240	–
Total debtors	2,540	–

Investment assets

10,000 CBF Church of England Investment Fund shares (market value)	20,000	19,500

Representing the R H Smith endowment fund – income for ordinary purposes.

Assets retained for the church's use (unrestricted funds)

Freehold house at 36 Church Road (purchase price on 5 November 1984)	59,000	59,000

Liabilities (designated Organ fund)

Organ cleaning and tuning carried out in December 2006	6,200	6,200

Other tangible assets Lawnmower from the estate of Mr Luke Titus (restricted fund)

NOTES

1. The financial statements of the PCC have been prepared in accordance with the Church Accounting Regulations 2006 using the R & P basis.
2. The following assets are recognized but not necessarily valued in the Statement of Assets and Liabilities: Movable church furnishings held by the churchwardens on special trust for the PCC and which require a faculty for disposal.
3. The expenses paid to clergy may include a small immaterial proportion, which relates to their function as PCC members. No other payments were made to PCC members.
4. The payments to missions and overseas relief agencies included £1,200 to CMS and £1,350 to Tear fund re the Southern Africa Famine appeal.

Approved by the PCC on 8 March 2007 and signed on their behalf by Revd Onesimus Og (PCC chairman) and Mrs Hannah Hosea (PCC treasurer)

Example: Receipts & Payments account using columnar basis

St Emilion's Church, Barchester – Financial statements for the Year ended 31 December 2006

	Unrestricted Funds	Designated Funds	Restricted Funds	Endowment Funds	**Total 2006**	Total 2005
	£	£	£	£	£	£
Receipts & Payments account						
Receipts						
Voluntary Receipts						
Regular Giving						
Planned giving	29,400	–	–	–	**29,400**	27,200
Collections and other giving	9,900	–	–	–	**9,900**	10,600
Income tax recovered	8,700	–	–	–	**8,700**	8,300
	48,000	–	–	–	**48,000**	46,100
Other voluntary receipts (note 5a)	2,700	–	4,450	–	**7,150**	7,050
Activities for generating funds (note 5b)	8,300	–	–	–	**8,300**	9,000
Receipts from Church activities (note 5c)	4,300	–	–	–	**4,300**	4,100
Investment income (note 5d)	650	250	950	–	**1,850**	1,600
	63,950	250	5,400	–	**69,600**	67,850
Payments						
Church activities						
Diocesan parish share	41,500	–	–	–	**41,500**	37,050
Other payments (note 5e)	19,850	–	1,750	–	**21,600**	21,300
	61,350	–	1,750	–	**63,100**	58,350
Excess of Receipts over Payments	2,600	250	3,650	–	**6,500**	9,500
Transfers between funds	(2,000)	2,000	–	–	–	–
	600	2,250	3,650	–	**6,500**	9,500
Bank current and deposit accounts 1 Jan.	4,300	3,300	13,400	–	**21,000**	11,500
Bank current and deposit accounts 31 Dec.	4,900	5,550	17,050	–	**27,500**	21,000
Statement of Assets and Liabilities						
Cash Funds						
Bank current account	400	–	–	–	**400**	350
CBF Deposit Fund	4,500	5,550	17,050	–	**27,100**	20,650
	4,900	5,550	17,050	–	**27,500**	21,000
Other Monetary Assets						
Local Authority grant for churchyard	300	–	–	–	**300**	–
Income tax recoverable (recd Jan. 2007)	2,240	–	–	–	**2,240**	–
	2,540	–	–	–	**2,540**	–
Investment Assets (note 3)						

20,000 CBF Church of England Investment Fund shares at market value	–	–	–	20,000	**20,000**	19,500
Assets retained for Church use (note 2)	59,000	–	–	–	**59,000**	59,000
Liabilities – Organ clean/tune Dec 2006	–	6,200	–	–	**6,200**	–

The attached notes on page 2 form part of these financial statements.

Approved by the PCC on 8 March 2007 and signed on their behalf by Revd Onesimus Og (PCC chairman) and Mrs Hannah Hosea (PCC treasurer)

NOTES

1. The financial statements of the PCC have been prepared in accordance with the Church Accounting Regulations 2006 using the Receipts & Payments basis.

2. Fixed assets retained for church use is the freehold house at 36 Church Street, purchased 5 November 1984, at cost. Assets recognized but not valued in the Statement of Assets and Liabilities include:

   lawnmower from the estate of Mr Luke Titus (restricted fund).

3. The Endowment fund, a donation in 1999 by R. H. Smith, has to be retained as a capital fund, but the income is for ordinary church purposes. It is invested in CBF Church of England Investment Fund shares.

4. The movements in designated and restricted funds during the year were:

	Bal. B/fwd	Receipts	Payments	Transfer	Bal. C/Fwd
Restricted: Church fabric (including tower)	13,400	5,050	1,400	–	17,050
Flower fund	–	350	350	–	–
	13,400	5,400	1,750	–	17,050
Designated: Organ fund	3,300	250	–	2,000	5,550

The Fabric fund represents accumulated donations and appeals for fabric maintenance, which can only be spent for that purpose.

The Flower fund represents a donation from a parishioner to be spent on Easter lilies in memory of her recently deceased mother. The cost of the flowers is included in costs of services.

The transfer to the Organ fund was from ordinary unrestricted funds to meet the balance of the clean/tune costs.

		Unrestricted Fund £	Designated Fund £	Restricted Funds £	**Total 2006 £**	Total 2005 £
5.	Receipts and Payments analysis					
(a)	Other voluntary receipts					
	Legacy	1,000	–	–	**1,000**	–
	Donations	1,700	–	4,450	**6,150**	7,050
		2,700	–	4,450	**7,150**	7,050
(b)	Activities for generating funds – receipts					
	Parish magazine – sales and adverts	2,200	–	–	**2,200**	2,100
	Rent – temporary let, Curate's house	3,700	–	–	**3,700**	3,700
	Summer fete and Christmas bazaar	2,400	–	–	**2,400**	2,500
	Rummage sales	–	–	–	–	700
		8,300	–	–	**8,300**	9,000
(c)	Receipts from Church activities					
	Fees	400	–	–	**400**	300
	Church Centre – local community use	3,900	–	–	**3,900**	3,800
		4,300	–	–	**4,300**	4,100
(d)	Receipts from investments					
	Bank and CBF Deposit Fund interest	150	250	950	**1,350**	1,100
	Dividend on CBF Investment Fund	500	–	–	**500**	500
		650	250	950	**1,850**	1,600
(e)	Church activities – payments					
	Overseas missions and relief					
	CMS	1,200	–	–	**1,200**	1,200
	Southern Africa Famine appeal	1,350	–	–	**1,350**	–
	Earthquake appeal	–	–	–	–	1,350
		2,550	–	–	**2,550**	2,550
	Church running expenses	5,200	–	–	**5,200**	5,300
	Clergy expenses	1,900	–	–	**1,900**	1,800
	Cost of services	2,600	–	350	**2,950**	2,100
	Buildings maintenance	2,500	–	–	**2,500**	5,200
	Lychgate roof repair	–	–	1,400	**1,400**	–
	Organ inspection	–	–	–	–	150
	Printing Magazine	1,800	–	–	**1,800**	1,800
	Printing and stationery	1,100	–	–	**1,100**	1,200
	Cleaning church centre	1,200	–	–	**1,200**	1,200
	Sunday school teachers training	1,000	–	–	**1,000**	–
		19,850	–	1,750	**21,600**	21,300

6. The expenses paid to clergy may include a small immaterial proportion, which relates to their function as PCC members. No other payments were made to PCC members.

Example: Accruals accounts, comprising SOFA, balance sheet and notes

Parochial Church Council of St Leger, Ambridge
Statement of financial activities

For the year ending 31 December 2006

	Note	Unrestricted Funds £	Restricted Funds £	Endowment Funds £	TOTAL FUNDS 2006 £	2005 £
INCOMING RESOURCES						
Voluntary income	2(a)	59,200	35,500	–	**94,700**	68,900
Activities for generating funds	2(b)	150	–	–	**150**	200
Income from investments	2(c)	3,250	2,500	–	**5,750**	6,250
Church activities	2(d)	1,600	–	–	**1,600**	900
Other incoming resources	2(e)	–	–	–	–	–
TOTAL INCOMING RESOURCES		64,200	38,000	–	**102,200**	76,250
RESOURCES EXPENDED						
Cost of generation voluntary income	3(b)	–	250	–	**250**	–
Fund-raising trading costs	3(c)	50	–	–	**50**	75
Church activities	3(a)	53,750	41,025	–	**94,775**	80,860
Governance costs		–	–	–	–	–
TOTAL RESOURCES EXPENDED		53,800	41,275	–	**95,075**	80,935
NET INCOMING RESOURCES BEFORE OTHER RECOGNIZED GAINS AND LOSSES		10,400	(3,275)	–	**7,125**	(4,685)
Gains on investment assets:						
on disposal	5(b)	5,000	855	–	**5,855**	–
on revaluation	5(b)	–	395	500	**895**	2,000
NET MOVEMENT IN FUNDS		15,400	(2,025)	500	**13,875**	(2,685)
BALANCES B/FWD 1 JANUARY		27,000	4,000	2,000	**33,000**	35,685
BALANCES C/FWD 31 DECEMBER		42,400	1,975	2,500	**46,875**	33,000

The notes on pages 3 to 7 form part of this account

Parochial Church Council of St Leger, Ambridge
Balance sheet at 31 December 2006

	Notes	2006 £	2005 £
FIXED ASSETS			
Tangible	5(a)	28,000	31,000
Investment	5(b)	12,000	3,315
		40,000	34,315
CURRENT ASSETS			
Stock		150	150
Debtors	6	850	1,000
Short term deposits		10,000	1,000
Cash at bank and in hand		1,000	1,985
		12,000	4,135
LIABILITIES			
Creditors – amounts falling due in one year	7	4,125	5,450
NET CURRENT ASSETS / (LIABILITIES)		7,875	(1,315)
Total assets less current liabilities		47,875	33,000
Creditors – amounts falling due after one year		1,000	–
balance of 2005 parish share deferred till 2008			
TOTAL NET ASSETS		**46,875**	**33,000**
PARISH FUNDS			
Unrestricted		42,400	27,000
Restricted	9	1,975	4,000
Endowment	9	2,500	2,000
		46,875	**33,000**

Approved by the Parochial Church Council on 23 March 2007 and signed on its behalf by

The Revd Canon Elisha Areopagus (PCC chairman)

The notes on pages 3 to 7 form part of these accounts

Notes to the financial statements

For the year ended 31 December 2006

1. ACCOUNTING POLICIES

The financial statements have been prepared in accordance with the Church Accounting Regulations 2006 together with applicable accounting standards and the SORP 2005.

The financial statements have been prepared under the historical cost convention except for the valuation of investment assets, which are shown at market value. The financial statements include all transactions, assets and liabilities for which the PCC is responsible in law. They do not include the accounts of church groups that owe their main affiliation to another body, nor those that are informal gatherings of church members.

Funds

Endowment funds are funds, the capital of which must be maintained; only income arising from investment of the endowment may be used either as restricted or unrestricted funds depending upon the purpose for which the endowment was established.

Restricted funds represent (a) income from trusts or endowments which may be expended only on those restricted objects provided in the terms of the trust or bequest, and (b) donations or grants received for a specific object or invited by the PCC for a specific object. The funds may only be expended on the specific object for which they were given. Any balance remaining unspent at the end of each year must be carried forward as a balance on that fund. The PCC does not usually invest separately for each fund. Where there is no separate investment, interest is apportioned to individual funds on an average balance basis.

Unrestricted funds are general funds which can be used for PCC ordinary purposes.

Incoming resources

Planned giving, collections and donations are recognized when received. Tax refunds are recognized when the incoming resource to which they relate is received. Grants and legacies are accounted for when the PCC is legally entitled to the amounts due. Dividends are accounted for when receivable, interest is accrued. All other income is recognized when it is receivable. All incoming resources are accounted for gross.

Resources expended

Grants and donations are accounted for when paid over, or when awarded, if that award creates a binding or constructive obligation on the PCC. The diocesan parish share is accounted for when due. Amounts received specifically for mission are dealt with as restricted funds. All other expenditure is generally recognized when it is incurred and is accounted for gross.

Fixed assets

Consecrated and benefice property is not included in the accounts in accordance with s.96(2)(a) of the Charities Act 1993.

Movable church furnishings held by the vicar and churchwardens on special trust for the PCC and which require a faculty for disposal are inalienable property, listed in the church's inventory, which can be inspected (at any reasonable time). For anything acquired prior to 2000 there is insufficient cost information available and therefore such assets are not valued in the financial statements. Subsequently no individual item has cost more than £1,000 so all such expenditure has been written off when incurred.

No cost information is available for the curate's house so it is included at a deemed cost being its 1994 valuation. It is being depreciated at £1,000 per annum with effect from 2003.

Equipment used within the church premises is depreciated on a straight-line basis over four years. Individual items of equipment with a purchase price of £500 or less are written off when the asset is acquired.

Investments are valued at market value at 31 December.

		Unrestricted Funds £	Restricted Funds £	Endowment Funds £	TOTAL 2006 £	FUNDS 2005 £
2.	**INCOMING RESOURCES**					
2(a)	**Voluntary income**					
	Planned giving:					
	Gift Aid donations	32,000	–	–	32,000	29,000
	Tax recoverable	10,200	–	–	10,200	9,100
	Other	2,900	–	–	2,900	3,250
	Collections (open plate)	9,900	1,600	–	11,500	13,000
	Gift days	700	–	–	700	500
	Grants	–	32,000	–	32,000	10,000
	Donations, appeals, etc.	250	1,900	–	2,150	50
	Legacies	3,250	–	–	3,250	4,000
		59,200	35,500	–	94,700	68,900
2(b)	**Activities for generating funds**					
	Fund-raising (coffee mornings)	150	–	–	150	200
		150	–	–	150	200
2(c)	**Income from investments**					
	Dividends and interest including tax recoverable	3,250	2,500	–	5,750	6,250
2(d)	**Income from church activities**					
	Church hall lettings	1,025	–	–	1,025	750
	Fees	575	–	–	575	150
		1,600	–	–	1,600	900
2(e)	**Other incoming resources**					
Total incoming resources		**64,200**	**38,000**	–	**102,200**	**76,250**
3.	**RESOURCES EXPENDED**					
3(a)	**Church activities**					
	Missionary and charitable giving					
	Overseas:					
	CMS	8,000	–	–	8,000	8,000
	Southern Africa famine appeal	1,500	–	–	1,500	–
	Earthquake appeal	–	–	–	–	1,500
	Support of Moses Cain and Grace Cross	–	40,000	–	40,000	23,000
	Home: Ambridge Pensioners Club	3,500	–	–	3,500	3,500
		13,000	40,000	–	53,000	36,000
	Ministry: Diocesan parish share	21,000	–	–	21,000	20,000
	Other ministry costs	4,500	–	–	4,500	6,000
	Church running and maintenance	6,000	–	–	6,000	8,000
	Depreciation curate's house and church equipment	3,000	–	–	3,000	3,000
	Sunday school leader training	1,500	–	–	1,500	2,000
	Parish magazine costs	250	–	–	250	150
	Churchyard upkeep	750	–	–	750	700
	Church hall running costs	3,250	1,000	–	4,250	4,500

	Printing and stationery	450	25	–	475	450
	Bank charges	50	–	–	50	60
		53,750	41,025	–	94,775	80,860
3(b)	**Generation of voluntary income**					
	Costs of appeals etc.	–	250	–	250	–
3(c)	**Fund-raising costs**					
	Coffee morning costs	50	–	–	50	75
	TOTAL RESOURCES EXPENDED	53,800	41,275	–	95,075	80,935

4. (a) STAFF COSTS

Wages and salaries	–	–	–	4,000	3,750

During the year the PCC employed an organist, gardener and church cleaner (all part-time) but no payments were large enough to attract social security costs.

Together these employees equate to less than one full time employee.

(b) PAYMENTS TO PCC MEMBERS

As the parish organist, Miss J Joshua, who is a member of the PCC, was paid £1,000 during the year. A small immaterial portion of the expenses paid to the incumbent may have related to his services as chairman of the PCC. No other payments or expenses were paid to any other PCC member, persons closely connected to them or related parties.

5. FIXED ASSETS

(a) **Tangible**

	(all unrestricted)	Freehold land and buildings	Church equipment	Total
		£	£	£
ACTUAL/DEEMED COST	At 1 January 2006	28,000	8,000	36,000
	Disposal	–	(3,000)	(3,000)
	Additions at cost	–	2,000	2,000
	At 31 December 2006	28,000	7,000	35,000
DEPRECIATION	At 1 January 2006	3,000	2,000	5,000
	Withdrawn on disposals	–	(1,000)	(1,000)
	Charge for the year	1,000	2,000	3,000
	At 31 December 2006	4,000	3,000	7,000

The freehold land and buildings comprise the curate's house at 1 Lazarus Rise, Ambridge.

Church equipment comprises office equipment. A photocopier was sold during the year for £2,000; its written down value was £2,000. It was replaced by a smaller machine, cheaper to run.

(b) **Investments**	£
Market value 1 January 2006	3,315
Disposal at carrying value	(3,315)
Purchases at cost	11,105
Revaluation gain	895
	12,000

At the beginning of the year, the ABC stock was sold and produced a gain of £5,855. During the year new investments have been made at various times in the CBF Church of England Investment fund. The holding at 31 December 2006 was 410 shares, which cost £11,105. The market value at 31 December 2006 represents investments for

Unrestricted funds	£7,525
Restricted funds	1,975
Endowment funds	2,500

		2006	2005
		£	£
6.	**DEBTORS (UNRESTRICTED FUNDS)**		
	Tax recoverable	750	650
	Prepayments and accrued interest	75	200
	Other debtors	25	150
		850	1,000
7.	**LIABILITIES**		
	Amounts falling due in one year (unrestricted funds)		
	Accruals for utility and other costs	2,000	2,500
	Other creditors	2,125	1,950
	Parish share	–	1,000
		4,125	5,450

8. **FUNDS**

The restricted funds comprise the Church Hall fund and the Mission fund. The latter represents funds raised for and grants received for the support of the mission work of Moses Cain and Grace Cross, members of the congregation working in the Far East.

The endowment fund is the Jericho bequest, which requires income to be spent on the running of the church hall.

Fund movements	Church hall	Mission
Balance at 1 January 2006	2,975	1,025
Incoming resources	150	37,850
Resources expended	(1,150)	(40,125)
Investment gains	–	1,250
Balance at 31 December 2006	1,975	0

9. **ANALYSIS OF NET ASSETS by fund**	Unrestricted funds £	Restricted funds £	Endowment funds £	TOTAL 2006 £
Tangible fixed assets	28,000	–	–	28,000
Investment fixed assets	7,525	1,975	2,500	12,000
Current assets	12,000	–	–	12,000
Liabilities				
Amounts falling due in one year	(4,125)	–	–	(4,125)
Amounts falling due after one year	(1,000)	–	–	(1,000)
	42,400	1,975	2,500	46,875

Example: Balance sheet on columnar basis

Parochial Church Council of St Leger, Ambridge
Balance sheet at 31 December 2006

	Note	Unrestricted funds £	Restricted funds £	Endowment funds £	TOTAL 2006 £	FUNDS 2005 £
FIXED ASSETS						
Tangible	5(a)	28,000	–	–	**28,000**	31,000
Investment	5(b)	7,525	1,975	2,500	**12,000**	3,315
		35,525	1,975	2,500	**40,000**	34,315
CURRENT ASSETS						
Stock		150	–	–	**150**	150
Debtors	6	850	–	–	**850**	1,000
Short-term deposits		10,000	–	–	**10,000**	1,000
Cash at bank and in hand		1,000	–	–	**1,000**	1,985
		12,000	–	–	**12,000**	4,135
LIABILITIES						
Creditors: amounts falling due in one year	7	4,125	–	–	**4,125**	5,450
Net current assets / (liabilities)		7,875	–	–	**7,875**	(1,315)
Total assets less current liabilities		43,400	1,975	2,500	**47,875**	33,000
Creditors – amounts falling due after one year– balance of 2005 parish share deferred till 2008		1,000	–	–	**1,000**	-
TOTAL NET ASSETS		42,400	1,975	2,500	**46,875**	**33,000**
PARISH FUNDS						
Unrestricted		42,400	–	–	**42,400**	27,000
Restricted	9	–	1,975	–	**1,975**	4,000
Endowment	9	–	–	2,500	**2,500**	2,000
		42,400	1,975	2,500	**46,875**	**33,000**

Approved by the Parochial Church Council on 23 March 2007 and signed on its behalf by the Revd Canon Elisha Areopagus (PCC chairman)

The notes on pages 3 to 7 form part of these accounts

NOTE: If the above format is used, note 9 shown in the previous example would not be required, and a number of references attached to individual notes identifying to which fund assets and liabilities belonged would similarly not be necessary.

An independent examiner's report
Example 1

Independent examiner's report to the PCC of St Emilion, Barchester

This report on the financial statements of the PCC for the year ended 31 December 2006, which are set out on pages 1 and 2, is in respect of an examination carried out in accordance with the Church Accounting Regulations 2006 ('the Regulations') and s.43 of the Charities Act 1993 ('the Act').

Respective responsibilities of the PCC and the examiner

As members of the PCC you are responsible for the preparation of the financial statements; you consider that the audit requirement of the Regulations and s.43(2) of the Act does not apply. It is my responsibility to issue this report on those financial statements in accordance with the terms of the Regulations.

Basis of this report

My examination was carried out in accordance with the General Directions given by the Charity Commission under s.43(7)(b) of the Act and to be found in the Church guidance, 2006 edition. That examination includes a review of the accounting records kept by the PCC and a comparison of the accounts with those records. It also includes considering any unusual items or disclosures in the financial statements and seeking explanations from you as trustees concerning any such matters. The procedures undertaken do not provide all the evidence that would be required in an audit, and consequently I do not express an audit opinion on the view given by the accounts.

Independent examiner's statement

In connection with my examination, no matter has come to my attention:

(1) which gives me reasonable cause to believe that in any material respect the requirements

- to keep accounting records in accordance with section 41 of the Act; and
- to prepare financial statements, which accord with the accounting records and comply with the requirements of the Act and the Regulations have not been met; or

(2) to which, in my opinion, attention should be drawn in order to enable a proper understanding of the accounts to be reached.

(Signed)

Mr Samuel Shadrach ACCA

43 The Glebe, Ambridge

23 March 2007

Explanation

The Regulations embody the provision of the Charities Act 1993, and the Charities (Accounts and Reports) Regulations promulgated thereunder, and The Statements of Recommended Practice issued by the Charity Commission. Section 43 of the Act allows an independent examination unless the PCC's gross income or total expenditure exceeds the audit threshold.

This means that the PCC has concluded that it is not required by law to have an audit by a registered auditor.

The Charities (Accounts and Reports) Regulations prescribe the contents of the independent examiner's report. This example of an unqualified report includes all the necessary information and the style may therefore be copied.

This means that the examiner has followed the Charity Commissioners' General Directions, which section 43(7)(b) of the Charities Act 1993 empowers them to make. Those Directions are repeated in Chapter 11 above.

The full text of section 41 of the Charities Act 1993 is given in Chapter 13 above. It explains that the records must contain entries showing from day to day all sums of money received and expended by the PCC, where they came from and on what they were spent so that accounts could be prepared at any time. The accounts and records must be preserved for six years.

This means that in all material respects accounts on the accruals basis have followed the Regulations and Chapter 8 above and are not contradicted by the Annual Report.

Examiner's qualified report

– failure to disclose information

(Example 2)

The following paragraph may be added to the statement to qualify it:

Independent examiner's qualified statement

The incumbent and PCC refused to provide information on a separately administered charity, the Jeremiah Trust, comprising a substantial endowment benefiting the PCC from time to time, and so it could not be ascertained to my satisfaction that the Trust should not be accounted for by the PCC. This matter gives me reasonable cause to believe that in this respect the accounts do not comply with the accounting requirements of the Act.

In connection with my examination, no other matter except that referred to in the above paragraph has come to my attention . . .

Example: Letter setting out agreed Terms of Engagement for the independent examiner

[Note: The phrases in square brackets should be omitted when the examination is of accounts on the receipts and payments basis.]

The Secretary of the Parochial Church Council
St Emilion's Church

Dear members of the PCC,

Engagement as independent examiner

The purpose of this letter is to set out in confirmation of our recent discussions the basis on which I am prepared to act as independent examiner to prepare a report in respect of the PCC's financial statements for the year ended 31 December 2006, and for future years until further notice, in accordance with section 43 of the Charities Act 1993 ('the Act') and the Church Accounting Regulations 2006 ('the Regulations').

Responsibilities of members of the PCC

As members of the PCC, you are responsible for maintaining proper accounting records and for preparing accounts which [give a true and fair view and] have been prepared in accordance with the Regulations.

You are also responsible for determining whether, in respect of the year (and the preceding two years), the PCC meets the conditions for exemption from an audit of the accounts set out in section 43(1) of the Act and the Regulations, and for providing me with information and explanations required for my examination.

Responsibilities of the independent examiner

I shall plan my work on the basis that an independent examiner's report on the accounts is required for the year, unless you inform me in writing to the contrary. As an independent examiner I have a statutory duty to state in my report whether any matter has come to my attention in connection with the examination which gives me reasonable cause to believe that in any material respect:

a) accounting records have not been properly kept in accordance with section 41 of the Act; or

b) the accounts do not accord with the accounting records or do not comply with the Regulations [other than in respect of the requirement for a true and fair view].

I also have a statutory duty to disclose in my report [inconsistencies between the accounts and the annual report and] matters coming to my attention in connection with the examination to which, in my opinion, attention should be drawn in order to enable a proper understanding of the accounts to be reached.

Should my work lead me to conclude that the PCC is not entitled to exemption from an audit of the accounts or should I be unable to reach a conclusion on this matter, then I will not issue any report and will notify you in writing of the reasons. In these circumstances, if appropriate, I will discuss with you the need to appoint an auditor.

Scope of the independent examiner's work

My work will be carried out in accordance with general directions setting out the duties of an independent examiner issued by the Charity Commission and as contained in the Church guidance.

My work as independent examiner will be a less onerous form of scrutiny than an audit of the accounts in accordance with Auditing Standards. My examination will include a review of the accounting records kept by the PCC and a comparison of the accounts presented with those records. It will also include a review of the accounts and consideration of any unusual items or disclosures identified. In such cases where I identify an unusual item, I will seek explanations from the PCC, and may carry out verification and vouching procedures where I require further clarification. [Similarly I will make assessments of the estimates and judgements made by you in your preparation of the accounts where they are material to the accounts.]

My work cannot be relied on to identify the occasional omission or insignificant error, nor to disclose breaches of trust or statute, neglect or fraud which may have taken place and which it is the responsibility of the PCC to guard against.

Should I become aware, for any reason, that the accounts may be misleading and we cannot agree appropriate amendments, and I then conclude that the matter cannot be adequately dealt with in my report, I will not issue any report and will withdraw from the engagement, and will notify you in writing of the reasons.

As part of my normal procedures, I may request you to provide written confirmation of any information or explanations given by you orally during the course of my work.

Fees

I am prepared to waive my fee for this examination.

Confirmation

Once it has been agreed, this letter will remain effective until it is replaced or until I cease to hold the position of independent examiner. I shall be grateful if you will kindly confirm your agreement to the terms of this letter by arranging for the signature, and return, of the attached copy, or let me know if the terms of this letter are not in accordance with your understanding of my terms of appointment.

Yours faithfully

Appendix

GS 1624

CHURCH ACCOUNTING REGULATIONS 2006

Made (Approved by the General Synod)	July 2006
Coming into force	1st August 2006

In pursuance of the power conferred by rule 54(8) of the Church Representation Rules the following Regulations are hereby prescribed by the Business Committee of the General Synod:

Definitions

1. In these Regulations:

"the Act" means the Charities Act 1993;

"the Charity Commission" means the Charity Commissioners for England and Wales;

"Council" means the parochial church council of a parish; and

"the SORP" means the Statement of Recommended Practice for accounting and reporting by charities published by the Charity Commission on the 4th March 2005 as from time to time amended, and any replacement Statement of Recommended Practice for accounting and reporting by charities published by the Charity Commission.

Revocation of the Church Accounting Regulations 1997 to 2001

2. The Church Accounting Regulations 1997 to 2001 shall continue to have effect in relation to accounts and annual reports of a Council for financial years ending on or before 31st December 2005 but, subject thereto, are hereby revoked.

Requirements in relation to accounts, audit etc

3. Subject to Regulation 4, a Council shall comply with its obligations under the Act (including any regulations made thereunder) and under the SORP with regard to:

(a) the keeping of accounting records for the Council;

(b) the preparation and preservation of annual statements of account for the Council;

(c) the auditing or independent examination of the statements of account of the Council;

(d) the transmission of the statements of account of the Council to the Charity Commission;

(e) the preparation of an annual report for the Council and its transmission to the Charity Commission; and

(f) the preparation of an annual return for the Council and its transmission to the Charity Commission.

4. If, in respect of a financial year of the Council, the accounts of the Council are not otherwise required by the Act to be audited or examined by an independent examiner, the accounts of the Council for that year shall be examined by an independent examiner; and such examination shall be conducted, and treated for all purposes, as if it were an examination required by the Act.

Commencement and citation

5. (1) These Regulations shall come into force on the 1st August 2006 so as to have effect in relation to accounts and annual reports of a Council for financial years ending on or after 31st December 2006.

(2) These Regulations may be cited as the Church Accounting Regulations 2006.

Index